Sup
Guide
to
Premier &
Football League
Clubs
1995

EDITOR
John Robinson

Eleventh Edition

British Library Cataloguing in Publication Data

A catalogue record for this book is available from the British Library

ISBN 0-947808-36-1

Copyright © 1994; SOCCER BOOK PUBLISHING LTD. (0472-696226)

72, St. Peters' Avenue, Cleethorpes, Sth. Humberside, DN35 8HU, England

Printed by Redwood Books, Kennet House, Kennet Way, Trowbridge, Wilts.

CONTENTS

FOREWORD

We are indebted to the staffs of the clubs featured in this guide for their cooperation and also to Michael Robinson (page layouts), Darren Kirk (cover artwork), Chris Ambler, Tom Morris and John Sambrooks (photos).

When using the guide, please note that 'child' concessions generally include senior citizens also. A number of clubs had not set their 1994/95 Season admission prices when we completed the guide and where this is the case we have shown 1993/94 price information.

Disabled Supporters should note that we have, in conjunction with Shoot! magazine, produced an entirely separate booklet, listing relevant information for all of the major League and Non-League clubs in Britain. This is priced at just 99p per copy and can be obtained post free from the address below.

Supporters of Non-League, Scottish and Welsh Football should note that we also publish
THE SUPPORTERS' GUIDE TO NON-LEAGUE FOOTBALL (priced £4.99)
THE SUPPORTERS' GUIDE TO SCOTTISH FOOTBALL (priced £4.99)
THE SUPPORTERS' GUIDE TO WELSH FOOTBALL (priced £4.99)
all of which are available, post free, from:

> Soccer Book Publishing Ltd. (Dept SBP)
> 72 St. Peters Avenue,
> CLEETHORPES,
> South Humberside
> DN35 8HU

Finally, we would like to wish our readers a happy and safe spectating season.

John Robinson
EDITOR

THE

NATIONAL FOOTBALL

STADIA

OF

BRITAIN

WELSH NATIONAL STADIUM

Re-Opened for Football: 31st May 1989
Location: Cardiff City Centre, CARDIFF
Telephone: (0222) 390111 (Ground)
Telephone: (0222) 372325 (F.A. of Wales)
Address: The National Ground, Cardiff Arms Park, Westgate Street, CARDIFF, Wales

Pitch Size: 110 × 69yds
Ground Capacity: 51,374
Seating Capacity: 42,355
(40,240 for Football Matches)

GENERAL INFORMATION
Car Parking: City Centre Car Parks
Coach Parking: By Police Direction
Nearest Railway Station: 5-10 minutes walk
Nearest Bus Station: 5 minutes walk
Nearest Police Station: Cardiff Centre
Police Force: South Wales
Police Telephone No.: (0222) 222111

GROUND INFORMATION
Family Facilities: **Location of Stand**:
Lower Tier of North & South Stands
Capacity of Stand: Not Specified

DISABLED SUPPORTERS INFORMATION
Wheelchairs: Accommodated in Disabled Section - North Side of West Stand - space for 24 wheelchairs
Disabled Toilets: Yes

ADMISSION INFO (1994/95 PRICES)
Adult Seating: £6.00 - £20.00
Child Seating: Half-price in Family Enclosures
Programme Price: £2.00
FAX Number: (0222) 343961
Note: Prices vary depending on the opponents & type of game.

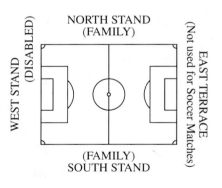

Travelling Supporters Information:
Routes: Exit M4 at Junction 29 and take A48(M) following signs for Cardiff City Centre (via A470). Use City Centre Public Car Parks.
From Cardiff Central Railway Station proceed past Bus Station, cross Wood Street and turn down Westgate Street (alongside the back of the Royal Hotel).

WEMBLEY STADIUM

Opened: 1923 **Location**: Wembley, Middlesex HA9 0DW **Telephone**: Box Office (081) 900-1234 **Telephone**: Administration (081) 902-8833	**Ground Capacity**: 80,000 **Seating Capacity**: 80,000 **Record Attendance**: 100,000 **Pitch Size**: 115 × 75yds

GENERAL INFORMATION
Guided Tours Available: Telephone (081) 902-8833 (ext. 3346)
Parking: Car Park for over 7,000 vehicles
Telephone Number: (071) 226-1627
Nearest Railway Stations: Wembley Park, Wembley Central, Wembley Complex (5-10 minutes walk)
Nearest Police Station: Mobile Unit in front of Twin Towers
Police Force Responsible for Crowd Control: Metropolitan
Police Telephone No.: (081) 900-7212

GROUND INFORMATION
All Sections of the Ground are Covered
Family Facilities: **Location of Stand**:
Radio 1 Family Enclosure, North Stand

DISABLED SUPPORTERS INFORMATION
Wheelchairs: Limited Facilities Available
Disabled Toilets: Yes
The Blind: No Special Facilities

ADMISSION INFO (1994/95 PRICES)
Admission £12.00 - £26.00; depending on the game and ground position. Also a £1 per seat booking fee
(Accompanied Children - half price in Family Enclosure)

OLYMPIC WAY & TWIN TOWERS
(ROYAL BOX SIDE)
NORTH STAND   FAMILIES

(STADIUM OFFICE END)
WEST TERRACE

(PLAYERS TUNNEL END)
EAST TERRACE

SOUTH STAND

How to get to Wembley By Road

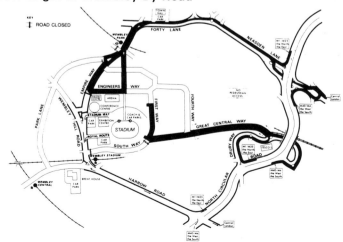

HAMPDEN STADIUM

Opened: 1903
Location: In the 'Mount Florida' area of Glasgow, South East of the River Clyde
Telephone: Administration (041) 632-1275
Address: Hampden Park, Mount Florida, Glasgow G42 9BA

Ground Capacity: 38,000
Seating Capacity: 38,000
Record Attendance: 150,239
(Scotland vs. England 17/4/37)
Pitch Size: 115 × 75yds
When development complete - capacity 60,000

GENERAL INFORMATION
Car Parking: Car Park for 1,200 vehicles
Coach Parking: Stadium Car Park
Nearest Railway Station: Mount Florida & Kings Park (both 5 minutes walk)
Nearest Police Station: Aikenhead Road, Glasgow G42
Police Force Responsible for Crowd Control: Strathclyde
Police Telephone No.: (041) 422-1113

GROUND INFORMATION
Family Facilities: **Location of Stand**:
Varies from game to game
Capacity of Stand: -

DISABLED SUPPORTERS INFORMATION
Wheelchairs: Accommodated in Disabled Spectators Terrace: 54 Wheelchairs, 48 Ambulance Seated, 120 Ambulance Standing
Disabled Toilets: Yes, by Disabled Area
The Blind: Personal Commentaries

NORTH STAND

WEST STAND

EAST STAND

(DISABLED TERRACE)
SOUTH STAND

MOUNT FLORIDA   KINGS PARK

Travelling Supporters Information:
Routes: From the South: Take the A724 to the Cambuslang Road and at Eastfield branch left into Main Street and follow through Burnhill Street and Westmuir Place into Prospecthill Road. Turn left into Aikenhead Road and right into Mount Annan for Kinghorn Drive and the Stadium; From the South: Take the A77 Fenwick Road, through Kilmarnock Road into Pollokshaws Road then turn right into Langside Avenue. Pass through Battle Place to Battlefield Road and turn left into Cathcart Road. Turn right into Letherby Drive, right into Carmunnock Road and 1st left into Mount Annan Drive for the Stadium; From the North & East: Exit M8 Junction 15 and passing Infirmary on left proceed into High Street and cross the Albert Bridge into Crown Street. Join Cathcart Road and proceed South until it becomes Carmunnock Road. Turn left into Mount Annan Drive and left again into Kinghorn Drive for the Stadium.

THE F. A. CARLING PREMIERSHIP

Founded
1992

Address
16 Lancaster Gate, London   W2 3LW

Phone
(071) 402-7151

THE ENDSLEIGH INSURANCE FOOTBALL LEAGUE

Founded
1888

Address
Lytham St. Annes, Lancashire   FY8 1JG

Phone
(0253) 729421

ARSENAL FC

Founded: 1886
Turned Professional: 1891
Limited Company: 1893
Admitted to League: 1893
Former Name(s): Royal Arsenal (1886-91); Woolwich Arsenal (1891-1914)
Nickname: 'Gunners'
Ground: Arsenal Stadium, Avenell Road, Highbury, London   N5 1BU

Record Attendance: 73,295 (9/3/35)
Colours: Shirts - Red with White Sleeves
          Shorts - White
Telephone No.: (071) 226-0304
Ticket Information: (071) 354-5404
Pitch Size: 110 × 71yds
Ground Capacity: 39,000
Seating Capacity: 39,000

GENERAL INFORMATION
Supporters Club Administrator: Barry Baker
Address: 154 St.Thomas's Road, Finsbury Park, London   N4
Telephone Number: (071) 226-1627
Car Parking: Street Parking
Coach Parking: Drayton Park (N5)
Nearest Railway Station: Drayton Park/ Finsbury Park
Nearest Tube Station: Arsenal (Piccadilly) Adjacent
Club Shop:
Opening Times: Weekdays 9.30-5.00
Sat. Matchdays 1.00pm onwards
Telephone No.: (071) 226-9562
Postal Sales: Yes
Nearest Police Station: 284 Hornsey Road, Holloway
Police Force: Metropolitan
Police Telephone No.: (071) 263-9090

GROUND INFORMATION
Away Supporters' Entrances: South Stand
Away Supporters' Sections: South Stand - Blocks 17 & 18
Family Facilities: **Location of Stand**: West Stand
Capacity of Stand: 2,000
ADMISSION INFO (1994/95 PRICES)
Adult Seating: £10.00 - £23.00
Child Seating: £5.00 (members only) - in Family Stand
Programme Price: £1.50
FAX Number: (071) 226-0329

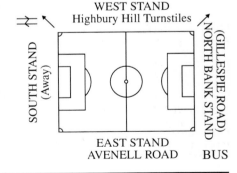

Travelling Supporters Information:
Routes: From North: Exit M1 junction 2 following City signs. After Holloway Road Station (6.25 miles) 3rd left into Drayton Park, after 0.75 mile right into Aubert Park and 2nd left into Avenell Road. From South:From London Bridge follow signs to Bank of England then Angel. Right at Traffic-lights to Highbury Roundabout (1 mile), into Holloway Road then 3rd right into Drayton Park (then as North). From West: Exit M4 Junction 1 towards Chiswick (A315), left after 1 mile (A40) to M41 the A40(M) to A501 Ring Road turn left at Angel to Highbury Roundabout (then as South).

ASTON VILLA FC

Founded: 1874
Turned Professional: 1885
Limited Company: 1896
Admitted to League: 1888 (Founder)
Former Name(s): None
Nickname: 'The Villans'; 'Villa'
Ground: Villa Park, Trinity Road, Birmingham   B6 6HE

Record Attendance: 76,588 (2/3/46)
Colours: Shirts - Claret + Narrow Blue Stripe
Shorts - White
Telephone No.: (021) 327-2299
Ticket Information: (021) 327-5353
Pitch Size: 115 × 75yds
Ground Capacity: Approximately 30,000 (all seater). Approximately 40,000 early 1995

GENERAL INFORMATION
Supporters Club Administrator: -
Address: c/o Club's Commercial Dept.
Telephone Number: (021) 327-5399
Car Parking: Aston Villa Leisure Centre Car Park, Aston Hall Rd.
Coach Parking: Opposite ground
Nearest Railway Station: Witton or Aston (5 minutes walk)
Nearest Bus Station: Birmingham Centre
Bus Services to Ground: 7/11/440
Club Shop:
Opening Times: Weekdays/Matchdays 9.30-5.00 (Closes for Match)
Telephone No.: (021) 327-2800
Postal Sales: Yes
Nearest Police Station: Queen's Road, Aston (0.5 mile)
Police Force: West Midlands
Police Telephone No.: (021) 322-6010

GROUND INFORMATION
Away Supporters' Entrances: All Seating - Witton End - R Block
Away Supporters' Sections: Witton End - R Block
Family Facilities: Location of Stand: North Stand
Capacity of Stand: 3,940

ADMISSION INFO (1994/95 PRICES)
Adult Seating: £12.00 or £14.00
Child Seating: £6.00 or £7.00
Programme Price: £1.20
FAX Number: (021) 322-2107

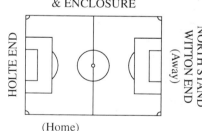

TRINITY ROAD STAND & ENCLOSURE

HOLTE END

NORTH STAND
WITTON END
(Away)

(Home)
DOUG ELLIS STAND

⇌ BUS →

Travelling Supporters Information:
Routes: From all parts: Exit M6 Junction 6 (Spaghetti Junction). Follow signs Birmingham (NE). 3rd Exit at Roundabout and in 0.5 mile, right into Aston Hall Road.
Bus Services: Service 7 from Corporation Street to Witton Square, also specials.

BARNET FC

Founded: 1888	**Record Attendance**: 11,026 (1952)
Turned Professional: 1891	**Colours**: Shirts - Amber with Black Collar
Limited Company: 1893	Shorts - Black + Amber Trim
Admitted to League: 1991	**Telephone No.**: (081) 441-6932
Former Name(s): Barnet Alston	**Ticket Information**: (081) 449-4173
Nickname: 'Bees'	**Pitch Size**: 113 × 72yds
Ground: Underhill Stadium, Barnet Lane,	**Ground Capacity**: 3,209
Barnet, Herts. EN5 2BE	**Seating Capacity**: 1,000

GENERAL INFORMATION
Supporters Club Administrator: c/o Club Shop
Address: c/o Club Shop
Telephone Number: -
Car Parking: Street Parking/ High Barnet Underground Car park
Coach Parking: By Police Direction
Nearest Railway Station: New Barnet (1.5 miles)
Nearest Tube Station: High Barnet (Northern) 5 mins.
Club Shop:
Opening Times: Wednesdays 10.30-2.30pm & Matchdays opens 2 hours before kick-off
Telephone No.: (081) 364-9601
Postal Sales: Yes
Nearest Police Station: Barnet (0.25 mile)
Police Force: Metropolitan
Police Telephone No.: (081) 200-2212

GROUND INFORMATION
Away Supporters' Entrances: Priory Grove
Away Supporters' Sections: East Terrace
Family Facilities: **Location of Stand**: Family Stand
Capacity of Stand: 200

ADMISSION INFO (1994/95 PRICES)
Adult Standing: £6.00 & £8.00
Adult Seating: £12.50 & £15 (£10 in Family Stand)
Child Standing: £2.00 & £4.00
Child Seating: £12.50 & £15 (£5 in Family Stand)
Programme Price: £1.50
FAX Number: (081) 447-0655

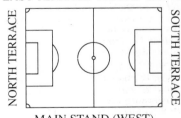

EAST TERRACE PRIORY GROVE
NORTH TERRACE
SOUTH TERRACE
MAIN STAND (WEST)
BARNET LANE

Travelling Supporters Information:
Routes: The ground is situated off the Great North Road (A1000) at the foot of Barnet Hill near to the junction with Station Road (A110).   Barnet Lane is on to the West of the A1000 next to the Cricket ground.

BARNSLEY FC

Founded: 1887	**Record Attendance**: 40,255 (15/2/36)
Turned Professional: 1888	**Colours**: Shirts - Red
Limited Company: 1899	Shorts - White
Admitted to League: 1898	**Telephone No.**: (0226) 295353
Former Name(s): Barnsley St.Peter's	**Ticket Information**: (0226) 295353
Nickname: 'Tykes'; 'Colliers'; 'Reds'	**Pitch Size**: 110 × 75yds
Ground: Oakwell Ground, Grove Street,	**Ground Capacity**: 11,631
Barnsley, S71 1ET	**Seating Capacity**: 11,631

GENERAL INFORMATION
Supporters Club Administrator: Mr.S.Curry
Address: c/o Barnsley F.C. Social Club, Oakwell Ground, Barnsley
Telephone Number: (0226) 287664
Car Parking: Queen's Ground Car Park (adjacent)
Coach Parking: Queen's Ground Car Park
Nearest Railway Station: Barnsley Exchange
Nearest Bus Station: Barnsley
Club Shop:
Opening Times: Weekdays 9.00-5.00 Saturday Matchdays 9.00-5.30; Saturdays with no home Matches 9.00-12.00
Telephone No.: (0226) 295353
Postal Sales: Yes
Nearest Police Station: Churchfields, Barnsley
Police Force: South Yorkshire

GROUND INFORMATION
Away Supporters' Entrances: West Stand
Away Supporters' Sections: West Stand
Family Facilities:
Accommodated throughout the Ground

ADMISSION INFO (1994/95 PRICES)
Adult Seating: Prices not fixed at time of publication
Child Seating: Prices not fixed at time of publication
Programme Price: £1.30
FAX Number: (0226) 201000

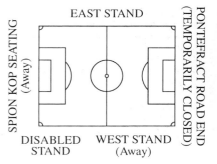

Travelling Supporters Information:
Routes: From All Parts: Exit M1 Junction 37 and follow 'Football Ground' signs to ground (2 miles).

BIRMINGHAM CITY FC

Founded: 1875
Turned Professional: 1885
Limited Company: 1888
Admitted to League: 1892
Former Name(s): Small Heath Alliance FC
(187-88); Small Heath FC (1888-1905);
Birmingham FC (1905-1945)
Nickname: 'Blues'
Ground: St. Andrew's, St. Andrew's Street,
Birmingham   B9 4NH

Record Attendance: 68,844 (11/2/39)
Colours: Shirts - Blue
　　　　　Shorts - Blue
Telephone No.: (021) 772-0101
Ticket Information: (021) 772-0101
Pitch Size: 115 × 75yds
Ground Capacity: 25,000
Seating Capacity: 25,000

GENERAL INFORMATION
Supp. Club Administrator: Linda Goodman
Address: 69 Malmesbury Road, Small
Heath, Birmingham
Telephone Number: (021) 773-5088
Car Parking: Coventry Road & Cattell Road
Car Parks
Coach Parking: Tilton Road
Nearest Railway Station: Birmingham New
Street or Birmingham Moor St. (20 mins walk)
Nearest Bus Station: Digbeth
Bus Services to Ground: 96 / 97 / 99 / 15 /
17 /58 / 60 / 900
Club Shop:
Opening Times: Weekdays 10.00-6.00
Saturday Matchdays 10.00-3.00 & 4.40-6pm
Telephone No.: (021) 766-8274
Postal Sales: Yes
Nearest Police Station: Bordesley Green
(0.5 mile)
Police Force: West Midlands
Police Telephone No.: (021) 772-1166

GROUND INFORMATION
Away Supporters' Entrances: City Stand
Away Supporters' Sections: City Stand
Family Facilities:　**Location of Stand**:
City End
Capacity of Stand: 2,343

ADMISSION INFO (1993/94 PRICES)
Adult Seating: £9.00 - £13.00
Child Seating: £5.00 - £6.00
Programme Price: £1.50
FAX Number: (021) 766-7866

CATTELL ROAD STAND

TILTON ROAD STAND

CITY STAND (Away)

ST. ANDREW'S STREET
STAND

REMPLOY
ENCLOSURE

Travelling Supporters Information:
Routes: From All Parts: Exit M6 Junction 6, to A38(M) (Aston Expressway), leave at 2nd exit then 1st exit at Roundabout along Dartmouth Middleway, after 1.25 miles take left into St. Andrew's Street.
Bus Services: Service 97 from Birmingham: Services 98 & 99 from Digbeth.

BLACKBURN ROVERS FC

Founded: 1875
Turned Professional: 1880
Limited Company: 1897
Admitted to League: 1888 (Founder)
Former Name(s): Blackburn Grammar School Old Boys FC
Nickname: 'Rovers'; 'Blues & Whites'
Ground: Ewood Park, Blackburn, Lancashire, BB2 4JF

Record Attendance: 61,783 (2/3/29)
Colours: Shirts - Blue & White Halves
Shorts - White
Telephone No.: (0254) 698888
Ticket Information: (0254) 696767
Pitch Size: 117 × 73yds
Ground Capacity: 30,000 (Approximately)
Seating Capacity: 30,000 (Approximately)

GENERAL INFORMATION
Supporters Club Administrator: Barbara Magee
Address: c/o Club
Telephone Number: (0254) 698888
Car Parking: Street Parking (nearby)
Coach Parking: By Police direction
Nearest Railway Station: Blackburn Central (1.5 miles)
Nearest Bus Station: Blackburn Central (1.5 miles)
Club Shop:
Opening Times: Weekdays 9.00-5.00 Saturday Matchdays 9.30-5.00
Telephone No.: (0254) 672137
Postal Sales: Yes
Nearest Police Station: Blackburn (2 miles)
Police Force: Lancashire
Police Telephone No.: (0254) 51212

GROUND INFORMATION
Away Supporters' Entrances: Darwen End
Away Supporters' Sections: Darwen End
Family Facilities: Location of Stand: Blackburn End - Upper Tier
Capacity of Stand: 3,000

ADMISSION INFO (1994/95 PRICES)
Adult Seating: £12.00 - £18.00
Child Seating: £6.00 - £18.00
Programme Price: £1.30
FAX Number: (0254) 671042
Note: Prices depend on category of match

(MEMBERS ONLY)
RIVERSIDE LANE
WALKERSTEEL STAND

KIDDER STREET
BLACKBURN END

DARWEN END
(Away)

JACK WALKER STAND
BOLTON ROAD

Travelling Supporters Information:
Routes: From North, South and West: Exit M6 Junction 31, or take A666, follow signs for Blackburn then for Bolton Road, after 1.5 miles turn left into Kidder Street.; From East: Use A679 or A677 and follow signs for Bolton Road (then as above).

BLACKPOOL FC

Founded: 1887
Turned Professional: 1887
Limited Company: 1896
Admitted to League: 1896
Former Name(s): Merged with Blackpool
St.Johns 1887
Nickname: 'Seasiders'
Ground: Bloomfield Road, Blackpool
Lancashire, FY1 6JJ

Record Attendance: 38,098 (17/9/55)
Colours: Shirts - Tangerine
Shorts - White
Telephone No.: (0253) 404331
Ticket Information: (0253) 404331
Pitch Size: 112 × 74yds
Ground Capacity: 9,701
Seating Capacity: 2,987

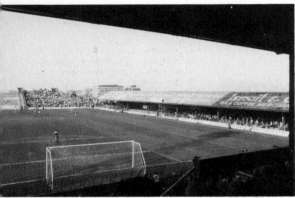

GENERAL INFORMATION

Supporters Club Administrator: Colin Johnson
Address: Blackpool Supporters' Club, Bloomfield Road, Blackpool
Telephone Number: (0253) 46428 (evenings only 7pm-11pm)
Car Parking: Car Park at Ground (3,000 cars) and Street Parking
Coach Parking: Mecca Car Park (behind Spion Kop)
Nearest Railway Station: Blackpool South (5 minutes walk)
Nearest Bus Station: Talbot Road (2 miles)
Club Shop:
Opening Times: Daily 9.00-5.30
Telephone No.: (0253) 404331
Postal Sales: Yes
Nearest Police Station: South Shore, Montague Street, Blackpool
Police Force: Lancashire
Police Telephone No.: (0253) 293933

GROUND INFORMATION

Away Supporters' Entrances: Spion Kop Turnstiles
Away Supporters' Sections: Spion Kop (Open) & East Paddock North Section (Covered)
Family Facilities: **Location of Stand**:
West Stand (South End)
Capacity of Stand: 400 (Family area)

ADMISSION INFO (1994/95 PRICES)

Adult Standing: £7.50
Adult Seating: £9.00 - £9.50
Child Standing: £4.00
Child Seating: £5.50 - £6.00
Programme Price: £1.20
FAX Number: (0253) 405011
FAMILY BLOCK: - Various additional discounts
1 Adult + 1 Child £10.50
2 Adults + 1 Child £18.00

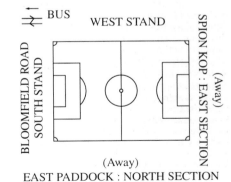

Travelling Supporters Information:

Routes: From All Parts: Exit M6 Junction 32 to M55. Follow signs for main car parks along new 'spine' road to car parks at side of ground.

BOLTON WANDERERS FC

Founded: 1874	**Record Attendance**: 69,912 (18/2/33)
Turned Professional: 1880	**Colours**: Shirts - White
Limited Company: 1895	Shorts - Blue
Admitted to League: 1888 (Founder)	**Telephone No.**: (0204) 389200
Former Name(s): Christchurch FC (1874-77)	**Ticket Information**: (0204) 21101
Nickname: 'Trotters'	**Pitch Size**: 113 × 75yds
Ground: Burnden Park, Manchester Road,	**Ground Capacity**: 20,000
Bolton BL3 2QR	**Seating Capacity**: 8,000

GENERAL INFORMATION
Supporters Club Administrator:
P. Entwistle
Address: 21 Woodfield, Bolton
Telephone Number: -
Car Parking: Rosehill Car Park (Nearby)
Coach Parking: Rosehill Car Park
Manchester Road
Nearest Railway Station: Bolton Trinity
Street (0.5 mile)
Nearest Bus Station: Moor Lane, Bolton
Club Shop:
Opening Times: Daily 9.30-5.30
Telephone No.: (0204) 389200
Postal Sales: Yes
Nearest Police Station: Howell Croft, Bolton
Police Force: Greater Manchester
Police Telephone No.: (0204) 22466

GROUND INFORMATION
Away Supporters' Entrances: Embankment
Turnstiles
Away Supporters' Sections: Embankment (Open)
& Covered Seating
Family Facilities: **Location of Stand**:
Great Lever Stand
Capacity of Stand: 3,000

ADMISSION INFO (1994/95 PRICES)
Adult Standing: £8.00
Adult Seating: £8.00 - £11.00
Child Standing: £5.50
Child Seating: £5.50 - £8.50
Programme Price: £1.30
FAX Number: (0204) 382334
FAMILY STAND: - Additional Discounts
1 Adult + 2 Children   £13.50
2 Adults + 2 Children   £18.00

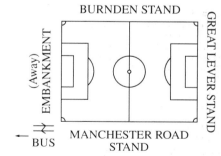

Travelling Supporters Information:
Routes: From North: Exit M61 Junction 5 or use A666 or A676. Follow signs for Farnworth (B653) into Manchester Road. After 0.5 mile turn left into Croft Lane; From South, East and West: Exit M62 Junction 14 to M61, after 2 miles leave motorway then 1st exit at Roundabout (B6536). After 2 miles turn right into Croft Lane.

AFC BOURNEMOUTH

Founded: 1890	**Record Attendance**: 28,799 (2/3/57)
Turned Professional: 1912	**Colours**: Shirts - Red and Black Stripes
Limited Company: 1914	Shorts - Black
Admitted to League: 1923	**Telephone No.**: (0202) 395381
Former Name(s): Boscombe St.Johns FC	**Ticket Information**: (0202) 395381
(1890-99); Boscombe FC (1899-1923)	**Pitch Size**: 112 × 75yds
Bournemouth & Boscombe Ath. FC (1923-72)	**Ground Capacity**: 11,880
Nickname: 'Cherries'	**Seating Capacity**: 3,813
Ground: Dean Court, Bournemouth, Dorset	BH7 7AF

GENERAL INFORMATION

Supporters Club Administrator: -
Address: Dean Court Supporters' Club
Bournemouth   BH7 7AF
Telephone Number: (0202) 398313
Car Parking: Car Park (1500 cars) Behind
Main Stand
Coach Parking: Kings Park (Nearby)
Nearest Railway Station: Bournemouth
Central (1.5 miles)
Nearest Bus Station: Holdenhurst Road,
Bournemouth
Club Shop:
Opening Times: Weekdays 9.30-5.30
Saturday Matchdays 9.30 to Kick-off
Closed on Wednesdays
Telephone No.: (0202) 311106
Postal Sales: Yes
Nearest Police Station: Boscombe (400 yds)
Police Force: Dorset
Police Telephone No.: (0202) 552099

GROUND INFORMATION

Away Supporters' Entrances: Main Stand Turnstiles
(Block A)
Away Supporters' Sections: Brighton Beach Terrace
(Open)
Family Room and Enclosure:
Family Block (Main Stand - F Block)
Capacity of Stand: 700

ADMISSION INFO (1994/95 PRICES)

Adult Standing: £6.00
Adult Seating: £7.50 - £9.50
Child Standing: £3.50
Child Seating: £3.50
Programme Price: £1.20
FAX Number: (0202) 309797

Travelling Supporters Information:
Routes: From North & East: Take A338 into Bournemouth and turn left at 'Kings Park' turning. Then first left at mini-roundabout and first right into Thistlebarrow Road for Ground. From West: Use A3049, turning right at Wallisdown Roundabout to Talbot Roundabout. Take first exit at Talbot Roundabout (over Wessex Way), then left at mini-roundabout. Go straight across traffic lights then right at mini-roundabout into Kings Park for ground.
Bus Services: Service 25 passes ground.

BRADFORD CITY FC

Founded: 1903
Turned Professional: 1903
Limited Company: 1908 (Reformed 1983)
Admitted to League: 1903
Former Name(s): None
Nickname: 'Bantams'
Ground: Valley Parade, Bradford   BD8 7DY

Record Attendance: 39,146 (11/3/11)
Colours: Shirts - Claret & Amber
　　　　　　Shorts - Black
Telephone No.: (0274) 306062
Ticket Information: (0274) 306062
Pitch Size: 110 × 80yds
Ground Capacity: 14,810
Seating Capacity: 6,500

GENERAL INFORMATION
Supporters Club Administrator:
Mrs J. Calvert
Address: 1 Westmoor Avenue, Baildon
BD17 5HG
Telephone Number: (0274) 591947
Car Parking: Street Parking and car parks
(£2.50 entry charge)
Coach Parking: By Police direction
Nearest Railway Station: Bradford
Interchange
Nearest Bus Station: Bradford Interchange
Club Shop: Yes
Opening Times: Monday to Saturday
9.00am-5.00pm
Telephone No.: (0274) 306062
Postal Sales: Yes
Nearest Police Station: Tyrrells, Bradford
Police Force: West Yorkshire
Police Telephone No.: (0274) 723422

GROUND INFORMATION
Away Supporters' Entrances: Midland Road
Away Supporters' Sections: Midland Road Standing
Family Facilities: **Location of Stand**:
N & P Stand
Capacity of Stand: 800 seated

ADMISSION INFO (1994/95 PRICES)
Adult Standing: £7.00
Adult Seating: £11.00
Child Standing: £1.00
Child Seating: £2.00 or £3.00 in the Family Stand
Programme Price: £1.20
FAX Number: (0274) 307457

MIDLAND ROAD
(Away)

SPION KOP

H.S.G. STAND

N & P STAND

Travelling Supporters Information:
Routes: From North: Take A650 and follow signs for Bradford. A third of a mile after junction with Ring Road turn left into Valley Parade. From East, South and West: Take M62 and exit Junction 26 onto M606. At end take 2nd left from roundabout and onto A6177 Ring Road. At next roundabout (3rd exit) turn right to City Centre (A614). At second roundabout turn right onto Central Ring Road (A6181) then left at next roundabout and left again at following roundabout marked 'Local Access Only'. Pass through traffic lights at the top of the hill following Keighley (A650) sign. Ground is then 0.5 mile along on the right.

BRENTFORD FC

Founded: 1889
Turned Professional: 1899
Limited Company: 1901
Admitted to League: 1920
Former Name(s): None
Nickname: 'Bees'
Ground: Griffin Park, Braemar Road, Brentford, Middlesex TW8 0NT

Record Attendance: 39,626 (5/3/38)
Colours: Shirts - Red and White Stripes
Shorts - Black
Telephone No.: (081) 847-2511
Ticket Information: (081) 847-2511
Pitch Size: 110 × 73yds
Ground Capacity: 13,870
Seating Capacity: 4,000

GENERAL INFORMATION

Supporters Club Administrator:
Mr. P. Gilham
Address: 16 Hartland Road, Hampton Hill
Middlesex
Telephone Number: (081) 941-0425
Car Parking: Street Parking
Coach Parking: Layton Road Car Park
Nearest Railway Station: Brentford Central
Nearest Tube Station: South Ealing
(Piccadilly)
Club Shop:
Opening Times: Monday-Friday 10.00-4.00
& also Matchdays
Telephone No.: (081) 560-9856
Postal Sales: Yes
Nearest Police Station: Brentford
Police Force: Metropolitan
Police Telephone No.: (081) 569-9728

GROUND INFORMATION

Away Supporters' Entrances: Brook Road
Away Supporters' Sections: Brook Road - Seats &
Terracing (Covered)
Family Facilities: **Location of Stand**:
Braemar Road - 'A' Block
Capacity of Stand: 640

ADMISSION INFO (1993/94 PRICES)

Adult Standing: £6.80 Member £7.80 Non-member
Adult Seating: £8.50 - £12.00 Member
£9.50 - £13.00 Non-member
Child Standing: £4.50 Member £5.50 Non-member
Child Seating: £6.50 - £10.00 Member
£7.50 - £11.50 Non-member
Programme Price: £1.50
FAX Number: (081) 568-9940

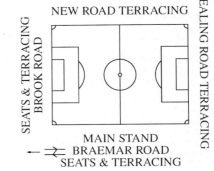

Travelling Supporters Information:
Routes: From North: Take A406 North Circular (from M1/A1) to Chiswick Roundabout and then along the Great West Road and turn right at the third set of Traffic lights into Ealing Road. From East: Take the A406 to the Chiswick Roundabout, then as North. From West: Exit M4 Junction 2 - down to the Chiswick Round-about, then as North. From South: Use the A3, M3, A240 or A316 to Kew Road, continue along over Kew Bridge, then right at the next traffic lights into Ealing Road.

BRIGHTON & HOVE ALBION FC

Founded: 1900
Turned Professional: 1900
Limited Company: 1904
Admitted to League: 1920
Former Name(s): Brighton & Hove Rangers
FC (1900-01)
Nickname: 'Seagulls'
Ground: Goldstone Ground, Newtown Road,
Hove, Sussex, BN3 7DE

Record Attendance: 36,747 (27/12/58)
Colours: Shirts - Blue & White Stripes
Shorts - Blue
Telephone No.: (0273) 778855
Ticket Information: (0273) 778855
Pitch Size: 112 × 75yds
Ground Capacity: 18,203
Seating Capacity: 5,274

GENERAL INFORMATION
Supporters Club Administrator: Liz Costa
Address: 72 Stoneham Road, Hove
BN3 5HH
Telephone Number: (0273) 778855
Car Parking: Greyhound Stadium and street
parking
Coach Parking: Conway Street, Hove
Nearest Railway Station: Hove (5 minutes
walk)
Nearest Bus Station: Brighton Pool Valley
Club Shop: Sports Express, Newtown Road
Opening Times: Weekdays 10.00-4.00
Telephone No.: (0273) 778855
Postal Sales: Yes
Nearest Police Station: Hove (1 mile)
Police Force: Sussex
Police Telephone No.: (0273) 778922

GROUND INFORMATION
Away Supporters' Entrances: Goldstone Lane
Turnstiles
Away Supporters' Sections: South East Corner (Open
Terrace); South Stand (Seats)
Family Facilities: Location of Stand:
South Stand - Entrance Newtown Road
Capacity of Stand: 1,500

ADMISSION INFO (1994/95 PRICES)
Adult Standing: £6.00
Adult Seating: West Stand £12; South Stand £8
Child Standing: £3.00
Child Seating: West Stand £6.00; South Stand £4.00
Programme Price: £1.30
FAX Number: (0273) 321095

Travelling Supporters Information:
Routes: From North: Take A23, turn right 2 miles after Pyecombe follow Hove signs for 1mile, bear left
into Nevill Road (A2023), then turn left at Crossroads (1 mile), into Old Shoreham Road. From East: Take
A27 to Brighton then follow Worthing signs into Old Shoreham Road. From West: Take A27 straight into
Old Shoreham Road.
Bus Services: Service 11 passes ground.

BRISTOL CITY FC

Founded: 1894
Turned Professional: 1897
Limited Company: 1897
Admitted to League: 1901
Former Name(s): Bristol South End FC
(1894-7)
Nickname: 'Robins'
Ground: Ashton Gate, Winterstoke Road,
Ashton Road, Bristol   BS3 2EJ

Record Attendance: 43,335   (16/2/35)
Colours: Shirts - Red
            Shorts - White
Telephone No.: (0272) 632812
Ticket Information: (0272) 632812
Pitch Size: 120 × 75yds
Ground Capacity: 19,815
Seating Capacity: 19,815

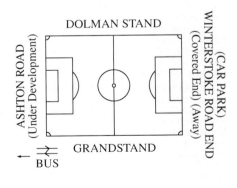

GENERAL INFORMATION
Supporters Club Administrator:
Mr. G. Williams
Address: c/o Club
Telephone Number: (0272) 665554
Car Parking: Street Parking
Coach Parking: Cannon's March
Nearest Railway Station: Bristol Temple
Meads (1.5 miles)
Nearest Bus Station: Bristol City Centre
Club Shop:
Opening Times: Weekdays 9.00-5.00
& Matchdays
Telephone No.: (0272) 538566
Postal Sales: Yes
Nearest Police Station: Kings Mead Lane
(2 miles) - Office at ground
Police Force: Avon/Somerset
Police Telephone No.: (0272) 277777

GROUND INFORMATION
Away Supporters' Entrances: Winterstoke Road
Away Supporters' Sections: Winterstoke Road -
Covered Area
Family Facilities: **Location of Stand**:
Dolman Stand
Capacity of Stand: 4,741

ADMISSION INFO (1994/95 PRICES)
Adult Seating: £8.50 - £11.00 (See note below)
Child Seating: £5.00 - £7.50
Programme Price: £1.00
FAX Number: (0272) 639574

Note: Admission prices may vary depending on the
League position of the team.

DOLMAN STAND

ASHTON ROAD
(Under Development)

WINTERSTOKE ROAD END
(Covered End) (Away)
(CAR PARK)

GRANDSTAND

← ⇄ BUS

Travelling Supporters Information:
Routes: From North & West: Exit M5 Junction 16, take A38 to Bristol City Centre and follow A38 Taunton
signs. Cross Swing Bridge (1.25 miles) and bear left into Winterstoke Road. From East: Take M4 then M32
follow signs to city centre (then as North & West). From South: Exit M5 Junction 18 and follow Taunton
signs over Swing Bridge (then as above).
Bus Services: Service 51 from Railway Station.

BRISTOL ROVERS FC

Founded: 1883	**Record Attendance**: 18,000
Turned Professional: 1897	**Colours**: Shirts - Blue & White Quarters
Limited Company: 1896	Shorts - White
Admitted to League: 1920	**Telephone No.**: (0272) 352508 or 352303
Former Name(s): Black Arabs FC (1883-84)	**Ticket Information**: (0272) 352508 or 352303
Eastville Rovers FC (1884-96)	**Pitch Size**: 110 × 76yds
Bristol Eastville Rovers FC (1896-7)	**Ground Capacity**: 8,880
Nickname: 'Pirates'; 'Rovers'	**Seating Capacity**: 1,006
Ground: Twerton Park, Bath, Avon	**Office**: 199 Two Mile Hill Rd., Kingswood, Bristol BS15 7AZ

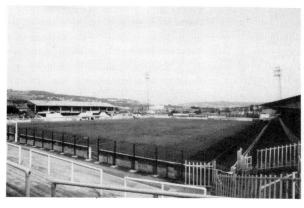

GENERAL INFORMATION
Supporters Club Administrator:
Mr. Steve Burns
Address: c/o Club's Office
Telephone Number: (0272) 510828
Car Parking: Very little space at ground -
(permit holders only)
Coach Parking: Avon Street, Bath
Nearest Railway Station: Bath Spa
(1.5 miles)
Nearest Bus Station: Avon Street, Bath
Club Shop:
Opening Times: Weekdays (Club Offices)
9.00-5.00pm, Saturdays 9.00am-1.00pm
Telephone No.: (0272) 352508 or 352303
Postal Sales: Yes
Nearest Police Station: Bath (1.5 miles)
Police Force: Avon & Somerset
Police Telephone No.: (0225) 444343

GROUND INFORMATION
Away Supporters' Entrances: Turnstiles 20/21
Away Supporters' Sections: Bristol End
Family Facilities: **Location of Stand**:
Family Enclosure Terrace - Bristol End
New Family Stand at side of Main Stand
Capacity of Stand: 236

ADMISSION INFO (1994/95 PRICES)
Adult Standing: £7.00
Adult Seating: £13.00 Main Stand   £9 Family Stand
Child Standing: £5.00
Child Seating: £8.50 Main Stand   £6 Family Stand
Away Fans: £7.00 - no concessions
Programme Price: £1.20
FAX Number: (0272) 353477
Family Enclosure: Adults £6.00   OAP's £4.00
Children £1.00

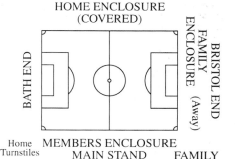

HOME ENCLOSURE
(COVERED)

BATH END

BRISTOL END FAMILY ENCLOSURE
FAMILY ENCLOSURE (Away)

Home
Turnstiles   MEMBERS ENCLOSURE
MAIN STAND   FAMILY
STAND

Travelling Supporters Information:
Routes: Take the A36 into Bath City Centre. Follow along Pulteney Road, then right into Claverton Street and along Lower Bristol Road (A36). Left under Railway (1.5 miles) into Twerton High Street and ground on left.

BURNLEY FC

Founded: 1882	**Record Attendance**: 54,775 (23/2/24)
Turned Professional: 1883	**Colours**: Shirts - Claret with Blue Sleeves
Limited Company: 1897	Shorts - White
Admitted to League: 1888 (Founder)	**Telephone No.**: (0282) 427777
Former Name(s): Burnley Rovers FC	**Ticket Information**: (0282) 427777
Nickname: 'Clarets'	**Pitch Size**: 114 × 72yds
Ground: Turf Moor, Brunshaw Road,	**Ground Capacity**: 21,290
Burnley, Lancs. BB10 4BX	**Seating Capacity**: 7,326

GENERAL INFORMATION

Supporters Club Administrator: David Spencer
Address: c/o Club
Telephone Number: (0282) 35176
Car Parking: Ormerod Road, adjacent to Fire Station (2 minutes walk)
Coach Parking: By Police direction
Nearest Railway Station: Burnley Central (1.5 miles)
Nearest Bus Station: Burnley (5 mins. walk)
Club Shop:
Opening Times: 9.15-5.00 Mondays - Saturday Matchdays. Friday Evenings 5-7pm Saturdays (no match) 9.15 - 1.00pm
Telephone No.: (0282) 427777
Postal Sales: Yes
Nearest Police Station: Parker Lane, Burnley (5 minutes walk)
Police Force: Lancashire Constabulary
Police Telephone No.: (0282) 425001

GROUND INFORMATION

Away Supporters' Entrances: Belvedere Road Turnstiles
Away Supporters' Sections: Covered Terracing
Family Facilities: **Location of Stand**:
Endsleigh Stand (Members Only)
Capacity of Stand: 4,166
Away Families: Community programme & visiting Junior Supporters Clubs

ADMISSION INFO (1994/95 PRICES)

Adult Standing: £7.00 or £7.50
Adult Seating: £9.50 or £11.50
Child Standing: £3.50 or £4.00
Child Seating: £4.50 or £6.00
Programme Price: £1.20
FAX Number: (0282) 428938

(Away End)
SKIPPERS LONGSIDE
COVERED TERRACING

BELVEDERE ROAD / ENDSLEIGH STAND

BEE HOLE LANE

BOB LORD STAND
BRUNSHAW ROAD

BUS

Travelling Supporters Information:

Routes: From North: Follow A682 to Town Centre and take first exit at roundabout (Ritzy Nightclub) into Yorkshire Street. Follow through traffic signals into Brunshaw Road. From East: Follow A646 to A671 then along Todmorden Road towards Town Centre. At traffic signals (crossroads) turn right into Brunshaw Road. From West & South: Exit M6 at Junction 31 and take A59 and then A677 towards Blackburn. Then follow A6119 (Blackburn ring road) to M65. Take M65 to Junction 10 and follow signs for Town Centre. At roundabout in centre take third exit into Yorkshire Street. Then as North.

BURY FC

Founded: 1885
Turned Professional: 1885
Limited Company: 1897
Admitted to League: 1894
Former Name(s): None
Nickname: 'Shakers'
Ground: Gigg Lane, Bury, Lancs. BL9 9HR

Record Attendance: 35,000 (9/1/60)
Colours: Shirts - White
Shorts - Navy
Telephone No.: (061) 764-4881
Ticket Information: (061) 764-4881
Pitch Size: 112 × 72yds
Ground Capacity: 13,000
Seating Capacity: 7,000

GENERAL INFORMATION

Supporters Club Administrator: P. Cullen
Address: c/o Club
Car Parking: Street Parking
Coach Parking: By Police Direction
Nearest Railway Station: Bury Interchange (1 mile)
Nearest Bus Station: Bury Interchange
Club Shop:
Opening Times: Daily 9.00-5.00
Telephone No.: (061) 705-2144
Postal Sales: Yes (Price lists available)
Nearest Police Station: Irwell Street, Bury
Police Force: Greater Manchester
Police Telephone No.: (061) 872-5050

GROUND INFORMATION

Away Supporters' Entrances: Gigg Lane
Away Supporters' Sections: Cemetery End
Covered Terracing/ B.Stand Seating
Family Facilities: Location of Stand:
Family Stand - Ron Wood Stand
Capacity of Stand: 1,800

ADMISSION INFO (1994/95 PRICES)

Adult Standing: £8.00   (£6.00 Members)
Adult Seating: £8 - £9   (£6.00 - £7.50 Members)
Child Standing: £8.00   (£3.00 Members)
Child Seating: £5.50 - £7.50   (£3 - £4.50 Members)
Programme Price: £1.20
FAX Number: (061) 764-5521

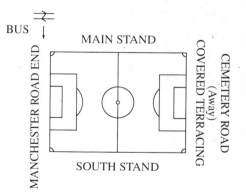

Travelling Supporters Information:

Routes: From North: Exit M66 Junction 2, take Bury Road (A58) for 0.5 mile, then turn left into Heywood Street and follow this into Parkhills Road until its end, turn left into Manchester Road (A56) then left into Gigg Lane. From South, East & West: Exit M62 Junction 17, take Bury Road (A56) for 3 miles then turn right into Gigg Lane.

CAMBRIDGE UNITED FC

Founded: 1919	**Record Attendance**: 14,000 (1/5/70)
Turned Professional: 1946	**Colours**: Shirts - Amber
Limited Company: 1948	Shorts - Black
Admitted to League: 1970	**Telephone No.**: (0223) 566500
Former Name(s): Abbey United FC (1919-49)	**Ticket Information**: (0223) 566500
Nickname: 'U's'; 'United'	**Pitch Size**: 110 × 74yds
Ground: Abbey Stadium, Newmarket Road	**Ground Capacity**: 10,205
Cambridge CB5 8LN	**Seating Capacity**: 3,415

GENERAL INFORMATION
Supporters Club Administrator: -
Address: c/o Club
Telephone Number: -
Car Parking: Coldhams Common (Do not park in the sidestreets)
Coach Parking: Coldhams Common
Nearest Railway Station: Cambridge (2mls)
Nearest Bus Station: Cambridge City Centre
Club Shop:
Opening Times: Weekdays 10.00-5.00 & Matchdays
Telephone No.: (0223) 566503
Postal Sales: Yes
Nearest Police Station:Parkside, Cambridge
Police Force: Cambridgeshire
Police Telephone No.: (0223) 358966

GROUND INFORMATION
Away Supporters' Entrances: Coldham Common
- Turnstiles 20-23
Away Supporters' Sections: South Terrace
(part covered - 360 seats/1,900 standing)
Family Facilities: Location of Stand:
Main Stand
Capacity of Stand: 200

ADMISSION INFO (1994/95 PRICES)
Adult Standing: £7.00
Adult Seating: £7.00 - £12.00
Child Standing: £4.00
Child Seating: £4.00 - £6.00
Programme Price: £1.20
FAX Number: (0223) 566502

```
         ELFLEDA ROAD
          MAIN STAND
        Disabled

NEWMARKET ROAD / NORTH TERRACE  [pitch diagram]  SOUTH TERRACE (Away)

          HABBIN STAND     Visitors Entrance
```

Travelling Supporters Information:
Routes: From North: Take A1 and A604 into City Centre, then take the A45. Turn off the A45 onto the B1047, signposted for Cambridge Airport, Horningsea and Fen Ditton. Turn right at the top of the slip road and travel all the way through Fen Ditton. Turn right at the traffic lights at the end of the village. Go straight on at the roundabout onto Newmarket Road. The ground is 500 yards on the left. From the South and East: Take the A10 or A130 into Cambridge and join the A45. Then as North. From West: Take A422 to Cambridge and join the A45. Then as North.
Bus Services: Services 180 & 181 from Railway Station to City Centre/ 182 & 183 to Ground.

CARDIFF CITY FC

Founded: 1899	**Record Attendance**: 61,566 (14/10/61)
Turned Professional: 1910	**Colours**: Shirts - Blue
Limited Company: 1910	Shorts - White
Admitted to League: 1920	**Telephone No.**: (0222) 398636
Former Name(s): Riverside FC (1899-1910)	**Ticket Information**: (0222) 398636
Nickname: 'Bluebirds'	**Pitch Size**: 112 × 76yds
Ground: Ninian Park, Sloper Road,	**Ground Capacity**: 21,403
Cardiff, CF1 8SX	**Seating Capacity**: 5,563

GENERAL INFORMATION

Supporters Club Administrator:
Kathy Shea
Address: Equity House, 6/7 Duke Street,
Cardiff CF1 1AY
Telephone Number: (0426) 950267 -
(messages only)
Car Parking: Sloper Road & Street Parking
Coach Parking: Sloper Road (Adjacent)
Nearest Railway Station: Cardiff Central
(1 mile)
Nearest Bus Station: Cardiff Central
Club Shop:
Opening Times: Weekdays 9.00-5.00
& Matchdays 1.5 hours before kick-off
Telephone No.: (0222) 398636
Postal Sales: Yes
Nearest Police Station: Cowbridge Road East
Cardiff (1 mile)
Police Force: South Wales
Police Telephone No.: (0222) 222111

GROUND INFORMATION

Away Supporters' Entrances: Grangetown End,
Sloper Road
Away Supporters' Sections: Grangetown End (Open)
Family Facilities: Location of Stand:
Below Grandstand and Canton Stand
Capacity of Stand: 3,271

ADMISSION INFO (1994/95 PRICES)

Adult Standing: Between £6.00 and £10.00
Adult Seating: Between £6.00 and £12.00
Child Standing: Between £3.00 and £5.00
Child Seating: Between £5.00 and £6.00
Programme Price: £1.00
FAX Number: (0222) 341148
Note: All prices vary depending on League position

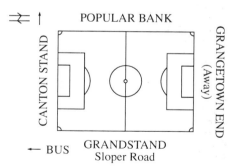

Travelling Supporters Information:

Routes: From North: Take A470 until Junction with Cardiff Bypass. Then 3rd exit at Roundabout A48 to Port Talbot, after 2 miles take 1st exit at Roundabout A4161 (Cowbridge Road). Turn right (0.5 mile), Lansdowne Road to Crossroads, turn right into Leckwith Road, then turn left (0.25 mile) into Sloper Road. From East: Exit M4 taking A48 to Cardiff Bypass (then as North). From West: Take A4161 Cowbridge Road (then as North).
Bus Services: Service No.2 - City Centre to Ground and Service No.1

CARLISLE UNITED FC

Founded: 1903
Turned Professional: 1903
Limited Company: 1921
Admitted to League: 1928
Former Name(s): Formed by Amalgamation of Shaddongate Utd FC & Carlisle Red Rose FC
Nickname: 'Cumbrians' 'Blues'
Ground: Brunton Park, Warwick Road, Carlisle   CA1 1LL

Record Attendance: 27,500 (5/1/57)
Colours: Shirts - Royal Blue
Shorts - White
Telephone No.: (0228) 26237
Ticket Information: (0228) 26237
Pitch Size: 117 × 78yds
Ground Capacity: 12,771
Seating Capacity: 2,151

GENERAL INFORMATION
Supporters Club Administrator:
M. Hudson
Address: c/o Club
Telephone Number: (0228) 24014
Car Parking: Rear of Ground via St. Aidans Road
Coach Parking: St. Aidans Road Car Park
Nearest Railway Station: Carlisle Citadel (1 mile)
Nearest Bus Station: Lowther Street, Carlisle
Club Shop:
Opening Times: Weekdays 9.00-5.00
Saturday Matchdays 10.00-3.00
Telephone No.: (0228) 24014
Postal Sales: Yes
Nearest Police Station: Rickergate, Carlisle (1.5 miles)
Police Force: Cumbria Constabulary
Police Telephone No.: (0228) 28191

GROUND INFORMATION
Away Supporters' Entrances: Turnstiles 22 to 25
Away Supporters' Sections: Visitors enclosure
Family Facilities: Location of Stand:
Main Stand
Capacity of Stand: 2,151

ADMISSION INFO (1994/95 PRICES)
Adult Standing: £6.00
Adult Seating: £8.00 or £8.50
Child Standing: £3.00
Child Seating: £4.00
Programme Price: £1.20
FAX Number: (0228) 30138

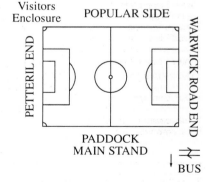

Travelling Supporters Information:
Routes: From North, South & East: Exit M6 Junction 43 and follow signs for Carlisle (A69) into Warwick Road. From West: Take A69 straight into Warwick Road.

CHARLTON ATHLETIC FC

Founded: 1905 **Turned Professional**: 1920 **Limited Company**: 1984 / PLC 1994 **Admitted to League**: 1921 **Former Name(s)**: None **Nickname**: 'Addicks' **Ground**: The Valley, Floyd Road, Charlton London SE7 8BL	**Record Attendance**: 75,031 (12/2/38) **Colours**: Shirts - Red Shorts - White **Telephone No.**: (081) 293-4567 **Ticket Information**: (081) 293-4567 **Pitch Size**: 112 × 73yds **Ground Capacity**: 14,950 **Seating Capacity**: 14,950

GENERAL INFORMATION
Supporters Club Administrator:
Steve Clarke
Address: P.O. Box 387, London   SE9 6EH
Telephone Number: (081) 304-1593
Car Parking: Street Parking
Coach Parking: By Police Direction
Nearest Railway Station: Charlton (2 mins walk)
Nearest Bus Station:
Club Shop:(081) 305-1289
Opening Times: Weekdays 10.00-6.00pm
Saturdays 10.00-2.45
Telephone No.: (081) 293-4567
Postal Sales: Yes
Nearest Police Station: Greenwich (2 miles)
Police Force: Metropolitan
Police Telephone No.: (081) 853-8212

GROUND INFORMATION
Away Supporters' Entrances: Valley Grove South
Away Supporters' Sections: Valley Grove South
Family Facilities: **Location of Stand**:
North Stand - Blocks A and B
Capacity of Stand: Not specified

ADMISSION INFO (1994/95 PRICES)
Adult Seating: £8.00 or £12.00 Members
          £10.00 or £14.00 Non-Members
Child Seating: £3.00 or £5.00 Members
          £5.00 or £7.00 Non-Members
Programme Price: £1.50
FAX Number: (081) 293-5143

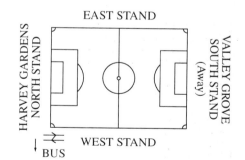

Travelling Supporters Information:
Routes: From North: Follow city signs from A1/M1, then signs for Shoreditch & Whitechapel to A13. Follow Tilbury signs and use Blackwall Tunnel to A102M. Branch left after 1 mile and turn left at T-junction into A206. Turn right 0.5 mile into Charlton Church Lane, then left into Floyd Road; From East: Take A2 to Eltham for Blackwall Tunnel (then as North); From West: Take M4, then A4 to Central London then signs to Westminster & Embankment - Take A2 Dover Road then A206 (Woolwich). Turn right into Charlton Church Lane, then left into Floyd Road.
Bus Services: Services 53, 54, 75, 177 & 180 from City.

CHELSEA FC

Founded: 1905
Turned Professional: 1905
Limited Company: 1905
Admitted to League: 1905
Former Name(s): None
Nickname: 'Blues'
Ground: Stamford Bridge, Fulham Road, London   SW6 1HS

Record Attendance: 82,905 (12/10/35)
Colours: Shirts - Blue
Shorts - Blue
Telephone No.: (071) 385-5545
Pitch Size: 114 × 71yds
Ground Capacity: Not yet known
Seating Capacity: Not yet known

GENERAL INFORMATION
Supporters Club Administrator:
Pippa Robinson
Address: Contact via Club
Telephone Number: (071) 385-5545
Car Parking: Street Parking
Coach Parking: By Police Direction
Nearest Railway Station: Fulham Broadway
Nearest Tube Station: Fulham Broadway
(District)
Club Shop:
Opening Times: Weekdays 10.30-4.30
& Matchdays
Telephone No.: (071) 381-4569
Postal Sales: Yes
Nearest Police Station: Fulham
Police Force: Metropolitan
Police Telephone No.: (071) 385-1212

GROUND INFORMATION
Away Supporters' Entrances: East Stand
Away Supporters' Sections: East Stand
Family Facilities: **Location of Stand**:
East Stand (North Side)
Capacity of Stand: 2,010

ADMISSION INFO (1993/94 PRICES)
Adult Seating: £10.00 - £30.00: Depending on class of game, place where seated, and whether or not you are members. Also special rates in a Family Section. Phone club for further details.
Child Seating: £7.00 - £8.00
Programme Price: £1.50
FAX Number: (071) 381-4831

EAST STAND
(Away)

NORTH TERRACE

SOUTH TERRACE

WEST STAND

Note: Much of the Ground is under reconstruction - stand names and sections may change.

Travelling Supporters Information:
Routes: From North & East: Follow Central London signs from A1/M1 to Hyde Park Corner, then signs Guildford (A3) to Knightsbridge (A4) after 1 mile turn left into Fulham Road; From South: Take A13 or A24 then A219 to cross Putney Bridge and follow signs 'West End' (A304) to join A308 into Fulham Road; From West: Take M4 then A4 to Central London, then signs to Westminster (A3220). After 0.75 mile turn right at crossroads into Fulham Road.

CHESTER CITY FC

Founded: 1884
Turned Professional: 1902
Limited Company: 1909
Admitted to League: 1931
Former Name(s): Chester FC
Nickname: 'Blues' 'City'
Ground: The Deva Stadium, Bumpers Lane, Chester CH1 4LT

Record Attendance: 5,638 (2/4/94)
Colours: Shirts - Blue and White Stripes
Shorts - Black
Telephone No.: (0244) 371376
Ticket Information: (0244) 371376
Pitch Size: 115 × 75yds
Ground Capacity: 6,000
Seating Capacity: 3,500 (Approximately)

GENERAL INFORMATION
Supporters Club Administrator:
B. Hipkiss
Address: c/o Club
Telephone Number: (0244) 371376
Car Parking: Ample at Ground
Coach Parking: At Ground
Nearest Railway Station: Chester (1.5 miles)
Nearest Bus Station: Chester (0.75 mile)
Club Shop:
Opening Times: 9.00-5.00pm weekdays and Matchdays
Telephone No.: (0244) 390243
Postal Sales: Yes
Nearest Police Station: Chester (0.75 mile)
Police Force: Cheshire
Police Telephone No.: (0244) 350222

GROUND INFORMATION
Away Supporters' Entrances: South Terrace
Away Supporters' Sections: South Terrace (Covered)
Family Facilities: **Location of Stand**:
Jewson Family Area - East Stand
Capacity of Stand: 100 seats

ADMISSION INFO (1994/95 PRICES)
Adult Standing: £7.00
Adult Seating: £9.00   (concessions in
Child Standing: £4.50   Family Enclosure)
Child Seating: £6.00
Programme Price: £1.20
FAX Number: (0244) 390265

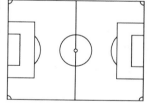

Travelling Supporters Information:
Routes: From North: Take M56/A41 or A56 into Town Centre then follow Queensferry (A548) signs into Sealand Road. Turn left at Traffic Lights by 'Texas' into Bumpers Lane - ground is 0.5 mile at end of road; From East: Take A54 or A51 into Town Centre (then as North); From South: Take A41 or A483 into Town Centre (then as North); From West: Take A55/A494 or A548 and follow Queensferry signs towards Birkenhead A494 and after 1.25 miles bear left onto A548 (then as North).

CHESTERFIELD FC

Founded: 1866
Turned Professional: 1891
Limited Company: 1921
Admitted to League: 1899
Former Name(s): Chesterfield Town FC
Nickname: 'Spireites'   'Blues'
Ground: Recreation Ground, Saltergate, Chesterfield   S40 4SX

Record Attendance: 30,968 (7/4/39)
Colours: Shirts - Blue and White
Shorts - White
Telephone No.: (0246) 209765
Ticket Information: (0246) 209765
Pitch Size: 112 × 73yds
Ground Capacity: 11,308
Seating Capacity: 2,608

GENERAL INFORMATION
Supporters Club Administrator: -
Address: c/o Club
Telephone Number: -
Car Parking: Saltergate Car Parks (0.5 mile)
Coach Parking: By Police Direction
Nearest Railway Station: Chesterfield (1ml)
Nearest Bus Station: Chesterfield
Club Shop:
Opening Times: Matchdays only
Telephone No.: (0246) 231535
Postal Sales: Yes
Nearest Police Station: Chesterfield (0.75ml)
Police Force: Derbyshire
Police Telephone No.: (0246) 220100

GROUND INFORMATION
Away Supporters' Entrances: Cross Street Turnstiles
Away Supporters' Sections: Cross Street End (Open)
Family Facilities: **Location of Stand**:
Main Stand - Saltergate Corner
Capacity of Stand: 400
Away Families: None

ADMISSION INFO (1994/95 PRICES)
Adult Standing: £6.00
Adult Seating: £7.00 - £8.00
Child Standing: £3.00
Child Seating: £3.50 - £4.00
Programme Price: £1.00
FAX Number: (0246) 556799

Travelling Supporters Information:
Routes: From North: Exit M1 Junction 30 then take A619 into Town Centre. Follow signs Old Brampton into Saltergate; From South & East: Take A617 into Town Centre (then as North); From West: Take A619 1st exit at Roundabout, (when into Town) into Foljambe Road and follow to end, turn right into Saltergate.

COLCHESTER UNITED FC

Founded: 1937
Former Name(s): The Eagles
Nickname: 'U's'
Ground: Layer Road Ground, Colchester CO2 7JJ
Record Attendance: 19,072 (27/11/48)

Colours: Shirts - Royal Blue & White Stripes
Shorts - Blue
Telephone No.: (0206) 574042
Ticket Information: (0206) 574042
Pitch Size: 110 × 70yds
Ground Capacity: 7,944
Seating Capacity: 1,150

GENERAL INFORMATION

Supporters Club Administrator: Pete Tucker
Address: c/o Club
Telephone Number: (0206) 574042
Car Parking: Street Parking
Coach Parking: Boadicea Way (0.25 mile)
Nearest Railway Station: Colchester North (2 miles)
Nearest Bus Station: Colchester Town Centre
Club Shop: At club, 2nd shop in Town Centre
Opening Times: At Club: Weekdays & Saturdays 10.30am-4.30pm
Town Centre: Monday-Saturday 9.00-5.30pm
Telephone No.: (0206) 574042 & 561180
Postal Sales: Yes
Nearest Police Station: Southway, Colchester (0.5 mile)
Police Force: Essex
Police Telephone No.: (0206) 762212

GROUND INFORMATION

Away Supporters' Entrances: Layer Road End Turnstiles
Away Supporters' Sections: Layer Rd. End (covered)
Family Facilities: **Location of Stand**:
Opposite Main Stand (Access from Layer Road)
Capacity of Stand: 1,508

ADMISSION INFO (1993/94 PRICES)

Adult Standing: £6.00 (Family Terrace £5.50)
Adult Seating: £6.50 - £8.00 (Family Terrace £8.00)
Child Standing: £4.00 (Family Terrace £3.50)
Child Seating: £4.50 (Family Terrace £4.00)
Programme Price: £1.00
FAX Number: (0206) 48700

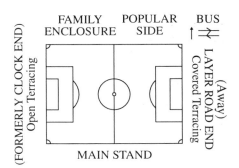

Travelling Supporters Information:
Routes: From North: Take A134/B1508 or A12 into Town Centre then follow signs to Layer (B1026) into Layer Road; From South: Take A12 and follow signs to Layer (B1026) into Layer Road; From West: Take A604 or A120 into Town Centre then follow Layer (B1026) signs into Layer Road.

COVENTRY CITY FC

Founded: 1883	**Record Attendance**: 51,455 (29/4/67)
Turned Professional: 1893	**Colours**: Shirts - Sky Blue/Navy & White Trim
Limited Company: 1907	Shorts - Sky Blue
Admitted to League: 1919	**Telephone No.**: (0203) 223535
Former Name(s): Singers FC (1883-1898)	**Ticket Information**: (0203) 225545
Nickname: 'Sky Blues'	**Pitch Size**: 110 × 76yds
Ground: Highfield Road Stadium,	**Ground Capacity**: 22,600
King Richard Street, Coventry CV2 4FW	**Seating Capacity**: 22,600

GENERAL INFORMATION

Supporters Club Administrator: The Secretary
Address: Coventry City Supporters Club, Freehold Street, Coventry
Telephone Number: -
Car Parking: Street Parking
Coach Parking: By Police Direction
Nearest Railway Station: Coventry (1 mile)
Nearest Bus Station: Coventry (1 mile)
Bus Services to Ground: C16/C35/C36/C37/ C7/C8/C24/C26/C27/C31A/C31C/C32/66/778
Club Shop: Thackhall Street
Opening Times: Daily except Sunday (Office hours)
Telephone No.: (0203) 257707
Postal Sales: Yes
Nearest Police Station: Little Park Street, Coventry (1 mile)
Police Force: West Midlands
Police Telephone No.: (0203) 539010

GROUND INFORMATION

Away Supporters' Entrances: Thackhall Street (Tickets from Away club)
Away Supporters' Sections: Mitchells & Butler Stand
Family Facilities: Location of Stand: Co-op Bank Family Stand
Capacity of Stand: 2,500

ADMISSION INFO (1994/95 PRICES)

Adult Seating: £6.00 - £19.00
Child Seating: £4.00 - £9.50
N.B. Prices vary depending on opponents
Programme Price: £1.30
FAX Number: (0203) 630318
Note: Children/OAPs pay adult prices unless members

BUS   (THACKHALL STREET)
MITCHELLS & BUTLERS STAND (Away)

FAMILY STAND
NICHOLL STREET
CO-OP BANK STAND

SWAN LANE
EAST STAND

MAIN STAND
(SOUTH SIDE)
KING RICHARD STREET

Travelling Supporters Information:

Routes: From North, West & South: Exit M6 Junction 2. Take A4600 and follow signs for 'City Centre'. Follow this road for approximately 3 miles and, just under railway bridge turn right at traffic lights into Swan Lane. Stadium on left; From East: Take M45 then A45 to Ryton-on-Dunsmore. Take 3rd exit at roundabout (1.5 miles) A423, after 1.25 miles turn right (B4110), follow to T-junction, left then right into Swan Lane.

CREWE ALEXANDRA FC

Founded: 1877
Turned Professional: 1893
Limited Company: 1892
Admitted to League: 1892
Former Name(s): None
Nickname: 'Railwaymen'
Ground: Gresty Road Ground, Crewe, Cheshire CW2 6EB

Record Attendance: 20,000 (30/1/60)
Colours: Shirts - Red
Shorts - White
Telephone No.: (0270) 213014
Ticket Information: (0270) 213014
Pitch Size: 112 × 74yds
Ground Capacity: 6,927
Seating Capacity: 1,869

GENERAL INFORMATION
Supporters Club Administrator: Glynn Steele
Address: 18 Gresty Road, Crewe
Telephone Number: (0270) 255206
Car Parking: Car Park at Ground (200 cars)
Coach Parking: Car Park at Ground
Nearest Railway Station: Crewe (5 mins.)
Nearest Bus Station: Crewe Town
Club Shop: At Ground
Opening Times: Monday - Thursday 9.00am-5.00pm & Matchdays 9.00am-5.00pm
Telephone No.: (0270) 213014
Postal Sales: Yes
Nearest Police Station: Crewe Town (1 mile)
Police Force: Cheshire
Police Telephone No.: (0270) 500222

GROUND INFORMATION
Away Supporters' Entrances: Gresty Road Entrances
Away Supporters' Sections: Gresty Road End
Family Facilities: Location of Stand:
Family Stand
Capacity of Stand: 650
Away Families: Yes

ADMISSION INFO (1994/95 PRICES)
Adult Standing: £6.00
Adult Seating: £8.00
Child Standing: £4.00
Child Seating: £5.50 (£2.80 in Family Stand - Junior Red Members Only)
Programme Price: £1.20
FAX Number: (0270) 216320

POPULAR SIDE
Disabled Section

GRESTY ROAD END (Away)

FAMILY STAND

MAIN STAND
Blind/Partially Sighted Area

Travelling Supporters Information:
Routes: From North: Exit M6 Junction 17 take Crewe (A534) Road, and at Crewe roundabout follow Chester signs into Nantwich Road. Take left into Gresty Road; From South and East: Take A52 to A5020 to Crewe roundabout (then as North); From West: Take A534 into Crewe and turn right just before railway station into Gresty Road.

CRYSTAL PALACE FC

Founded: 1905
Turned Professional: 1905
Limited Company: 1905
Admitted to League: 1920
Former Name(s): None
Nickname: 'Eagles'
Ground: Selhurst Park, London,   SE25 6PU

Record Attendance: 51,482 (11/5/79)
Colours: Shirts - Red with Blue Stripes
Shorts - Red
Telephone No.: (081) 653-1000
Ticket Information: (081) 771-8841
Pitch Size: 110×74yds
Ground Capacity: 18,103
Seating Capacity: 18,103

GENERAL INFORMATION
Supporters Club Administrator: -
Address: -
Telephone Number: -
Car Parking: Street Parking/Sainsbury Car Park near Ground
Coach Parking: Thornton Heath
Nearest Railway Station: Selhurst/Norwood Junction/Thornton Heath
Nearest Bus Station: Norwood Junction
Club Shop:
Opening Times: Weekdays & Matchdays 9.30-5.30
Telephone No.: (081) 653-5584
Postal Sales: Yes
Nearest Police Station: South Norwood (15 minutes walk)
Police Force: Metropolitan
Police Telephone No.: (081) 653-8568

GROUND INFORMATION
Away Supporters' Entrances: Park Road
Away Supporters' Sections: Park Road Corner - (Covered Seating)
Family Facilities: Location of Stand: Members Stand (Clifton Road End)
Capacity of Stand: -

ADMISSION INFO (1994/95 PRICES)
Adult Seating: £16.00 to £20.00
Child Seating: £12.00 to £15.00
Programme Price: £1.30
FAX Number: (081) 771-5311

Note: Prices vary depending on the game

Travelling Supporters Information:
Routes: From North: Take M1/A1 to North Circular (A406) to Chiswick. Take South Circular (A205) to Wandsworth, take A3 to A214 and follow signs to Streatham to A23. Turn left onto B273 (1 mile), follow to end and turn left into High Street and into Whitehorse Lane; From East: Take A232 (Croydon Road) to Shirley and join A215 (Northwood Road), after 2.25 miles take left into Whitehorse Lane; From South: Take A23 and follow signs Crystal Palace B266 through Thornton Heath into Whitehorse Lane; From West: Take M4 to Chiswick (then as North).

DARLINGTON FC

Founded: 1883	**Record Attendance**: 21,023 (14/11/60)
Turned Professional: 1908	**Colours**: Shirts - White/Black
Limited Company: 1891	Shorts - Black
Admitted to League: 1921	**Telephone No.**: (0325) 465097
Former Name(s): None	**Ticket Information**: (0325) 465097
Nickname: 'Quakers'	**Pitch Size**: 110 × 74yds
Ground: Feethams Ground, Darlington	**Ground Capacity**: 5,006
DL1 5JB	**Seating Capacity**: 1,105

GENERAL INFORMATION
Supporters Club Administrator: K. Davies
Address: 60 Harrison Terrace, Darlington
Telephone Number: (0325) 350161
Car Parking: Street Parking
Coach Parking: By Police direction
Nearest Railway Station: Darlington
Nearest Bus Station: Darlington Central
Club Shop:
Opening Times: Monday-Friday 9.00-5.00
Telephone No.: (0325) 465097
Postal Sales: Yes
Nearest Police Station: Park Police Station, Darlington (0.25 mile)
Police Force: Durham
Police Telephone No.: (0325) 467681

GROUND INFORMATION
Away Supporters' Entrances: Polam Lane Turnstiles
Away Supporters' Sections: West Terrace - Open
Family Facilities: **Location of Stand**:
West Stand
Capacity of Stand: 560
Away Families: Yes

ADMISSION INFO (1994/95 PRICES)
Adult Standing: £6.00
Adult Seating: £8.00   (£7.50 in Family Stand)
Child Standing: £3.00
Child Seating: £5.00   (£3.50 in Family Stand)
Programme Price: £1.00
FAX Number: (0325) 381377

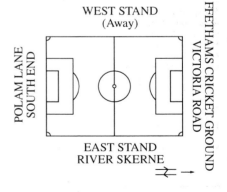

Travelling Supporters Information:
Routes: From North: Take A1(M) to A167 and follow road to Town Centre, then follow Northallerton signs to Victoria Road; From East: Take A67 to Town Centre (then as North); From South: Take A1(M) A66(M) into Town Centre and 3rd exit at second roundabout into Victoria Road; From West: Take A67 into Town Centre and 3rd exit at roundabout into Victoria Road.

DERBY COUNTY FC

Founded: 1884	**Record Attendance**: 41,826 (20/9/69)
Turned Professional: 1884	**Colours**: Shirts - White
Limited Company: 1896	Shorts - Black
Admitted to League: 1888 (Founder)	**Telephone No.**: (0332) 340105
Former Name(s): None	**Ticket Information**: (0332) 340105
Nickname: 'Rams'	**Pitch Size**: 110 × 71yds
Ground: Baseball Ground, Shaftesbury	**Ground Capacity**: 19,500
Crescent, Derby DE23 8NB	**Seating Capacity**: 15,000

GENERAL INFORMATION

Supporters Club Administrator:
Mr. E. Hallam
Address: c/o Club
Telephone Number: (0332) 340105
Car Parking: Numerous Car Parks within
0.5 mile
Coach Parking: Russel St. Derby
Nearest Railway Station: Derby Midland
(1 mile) and Ramsline Halt (specials only)
Nearest Bus Station: Derby Central
Club Shop:
Opening Times: Weekdays 9.30-5.00
& Matches
Telephone No.: (0332) 292081
Postal Sales: Yes
Nearest Police Station: Cotton Lane, Derby
Police Force: Derbyshire
Police Telephone No.: (0332) 290100

GROUND INFORMATION

Away Supporters' Entrances: Turnstiles 48-52
Away Supporters' Sections: Popular Side Terrace
Family Facilities: **Location of Stand**:
Vulcan Street End
Capacity of Stand: 3,500

ADMISSION INFO (1994/95 PRICES)

Adult Standing: £7.00
Adult Seating: £8.00 - £12.00
Child Standing: £4.00
Child Seating: £6.00
Programme Price: £1.40
FAX Number: (0332) 293514

```
                 TOYOTA STAND
              POPULAR SIDE TERRACE
               (Away)      (Home)

  O                                         V N
  S                                         U O
  M                                         L R
  A                                         C M
  S                                         A A
  T                                         N N
  O                                         T
  N                                         S O
                                            T N
  S                                         R
  T                                         E S
  A                                         E T
  N                                         T A
  D                                         N
  S                                         D
             SHAFTESBURY CRESCENT  S
```

Travelling Supporters Information:
Routes: From North: Take A38 into City Centre then follow signs Melbourne (A514), turn right before Railway Bridge into Shaftesbury Street; From South, East & West: Take Derby Ring Road to Junction with A514 and follow signs to City Centre into Osmaston Road, after 1.25 miles take left turn into Shaftesbury Street.
Bus Services: Services 159, 188 and 189 pass near the Ground. Some Special services.

DONCASTER ROVERS FC

Founded: 1879
Turned Professional: 1885
Limited Company: 1920
Admitted to League: 1901
Former Name(s): None
Nickname: 'Rovers'
Ground: Belle Vue, Bawtry Road,
Doncaster   DN4 5HT

Record Attendance: 37,149 (2/10/48)
Colours: Shirts - Red
            Shorts - Red
Telephone No.: (0302) 539441
Ticket Information: (0302) 539441
Pitch Size: 110 × 76yds
Ground Capacity: 7,794
Seating Capacity: 1,259

GENERAL INFORMATION
Supporters Club Administrator: K.Avis
Address: 64 Harrowden Road, Wheatley,
Doncaster
Telephone Number: (0302) 365440
Car Parking: Large Car Park at Ground
Coach Parking: Car Park at Ground
Nearest Railway Station: Doncaster (1.5m)
Nearest Bus Station: Doncaster
Club Shop:
Opening Times: Monday & Thursday 10.00-
12.30. Matchdays: 1 hour before & after game
Telephone No.: (0302) 539441
Postal Sales: Yes
Nearest Police Station: College Road,
Doncaster
Police Force: South Yorkshire
Police Telephone No.: (0302) 366744

GROUND INFORMATION
Away Supporters' Entrances: Turnstiles A &
1, 2, 3, 4, 'A' Block
Away Supporters' Sections: Rossington Road
(Open) & Main Stand, 'A' Block
Family Facilities: **Location of Stand**:
Main Stand
Capacity of Stand: -

ADMISSION INFO (1994/95 PRICES)
Adult Standing: £7.00
Adult Seating: £9.00
Child Standing: £3.50
Child Seating: £5.00
Programme Price: £1.00
FAX Number: (0302) 539679

POPULAR SIDE STAND

ROSSINGTON END
(Away)

Enclosure   BUS
MAIN STAND
BAWTRY ROAD

Travelling Supporters Information:
Routes: From North: Take A1 to A638 into Town Centre, follow signs to Bawtry (A638), after 1.25 miles
take 3rd exit from roundabout into Bawtry Road; From East: Take M18 to A630, after 2.75 miles take 1st
exit at roundabout into A18, after 2.5 miles take 1st exit at roundabout into Bawtry Road; From South: Take
M1 then M18, to A6182. After 2 miles 3rd exit at roundabout S/P 'Scunthorpe A18'. Then after 1.25 miles
take 3rd exit at roundabout into Bawtry Road; From West: Take A635 into Town Centre and follow signs
'Bawtry' (then as South).

EVERTON FC

Founded: 1878	**Record Attendance**: 78,299 (18/9/48)
Turned Professional: 1885	**Colours**: Shirts - Blue
Limited Company: 1892	Shorts - White
Admitted to League: 1888 (Founder)	**Telephone No.**: (051) 521-2020
Former Name(s): St. Domingo's FC (1878-79)	**Ticket Information**: (051) 523-6666
Nickname: 'Blues' 'Toffeemen'	**Pitch Size**: 112 × 78yds
Ground: Goodison Park, Goodison Road.	**Ground Capacity**: 40,000
Liverpool L4 4EL	**Seating Capacity**: 40,000

GENERAL INFORMATION

Supporters Club Administrator: The Secretary
Address: -
Telephone Number: (051) 523-1614
Car Parking: Corner of Priory and Utting Av.
Coach Parking: Priory Road
Nearest Railway Station: Liverpool Lime Street
Nearest Bus Station: Brownlow Hill, Liverpool
Club Shop:
Opening Times: Weekdays & Matchdays 9.30-4.30 and Evening matches
Telephone No.: (051) 521-2020 ext. 2253
Postal Sales: Yes - Mail Order & Credit Card
Nearest Police Station: Walton Lane, Liverpool
Police Force: Merseyside
Police Telephone No.: (051) 709-6010

GROUND INFORMATION

Away Supporters' Entrances: Bullens Road
Away Supporters' Sections: Bullens Stand
Family Facilities: Location of Stand: In front of Main Stand
Capacity of Stand: 2,080

ADMISSION INFO (1994/95 PRICES)

Adult Seating: £9.00 - £14.00
Child Seating: £4.00 - £6.00
Programme Price: £1.40
FAX Number: (051) 523-9666
Note : Prices vary depending on the opponents

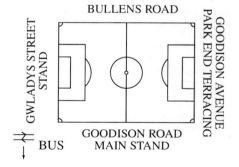

Travelling Supporters Information:

Routes: From North: Exit M6 junction 24. Take A58 Liverpool Road to A580 and follow into Walton Hall Avenue; From South & East: Exit M6 junction 21A to M62. At end of M62 turn right into Queen's Drive. After 3.75 miles turn left into Walton Hall Avenue; From North Wales: Cross Mersey into City Centre and follow signs to Preston (A580) into Walton Hall Avenue.
Bus Services: Service from City Centre - 19, 20, 21, F1, F9, F2, 30

EXETER CITY FC

Founded: 1904
Turned Professional: 1908
Limited Company: 1908
Admitted to League: 1920
Former Name(s): Formed by amalgamation of
St. Sidwell United FC & Exeter United FC
Nickname: 'Grecians'
Ground: St. James Park, Exeter EX4 6PX

Record Attendance: 20,984 (4/3/31)
Colours: Shirts - Red & White Stripes
Shorts - White
Telephone No.: (0392) 54073
Ticket Information: (0392) 54073
Pitch Size: 114 × 73yds
Ground Capacity: 10,570
Seating Capacity: 1,690

GENERAL INFORMATION
Supporters Club Administrator: -
Address: c/o Club
Telephone Number: (0392) 54073
Car Parking: King William Street
Coach Parking: Paris Street Bus Station
Nearest Railway Station: Exeter St. James
Park (Adjacent)
Nearest Bus Station: Paris Street Bus Station
Club Shop:
Opening Times: Weekdays & Matchdays
9.00-5.00pm
Telephone No.: (0392) 54073
Postal Sales: Yes
Nearest Police Station: Heavitree Road,
Exeter (0.5 mile)
Police Force: Devon & Cornwall
Police Telephone No.: (0392) 52101

GROUND INFORMATION
Away Supporters' Entrances: St. James Road Turn-
stiles
Away Supporters' Sections: St.James Road Enclosure
Family Facilities: Location of Stand:
Block C - Grandstand
Capacity of Stand: -

ADMISSION INFO (1994/95 PRICES)
Adult Standing: £5.00 - £6.00
Adult Seating: £8.00
Child Standing: £3.00
Child Seating: £5.00
Programme Price: £1.30
FAX Number: (0392) 425885

```
         OLD TIVERTON ROAD END          COWSHED          ST. JAMES ROAD
              BIG BANK                                       (Away)

                              MAIN GRANDSTAND
                               WELL STREET
```

Travelling Supporters Information:
Routes: From North: Exit M5 junction 30 and follow signs to City Centre along Sidmouth Road and onto
Heavitree Road, take 4th exit at roundabout into Western Way and 2nd exit Tiverton Road, next left into St.
James Road; From East: Take A30 into Heavitree Road (then as North); From South & West: Take A38
and follow City Centre signs into Western Way and 3rd exit at roundabout into St. James Road.
Bus Services: Services A, D, J, K & S from City Centre,

FULHAM FC

Founded: 1879
Turned Professional: 1898
Limited Company: 1903
Admitted to League: 1907
Former Name(s): Fulham St. Andrew's FC (1879-1898)
Nickname: 'Cottagers'
Ground: Craven Cottage, Stevenage Road, Fulham, London SW6 6HH

Record Attendance: 49,335 (8/10/38)
Colours: Shirts - White
Shorts - Black
Telephone No.: (071) 736-6561
Ticket Information: (071) 736-6561
Pitch Size: 110 × 75yds
Ground Capacity: 10,400
Seating Capacity: 4,100

GENERAL INFORMATION

Supporters Club Administrator: The Chairman
Address: c/o The Club
Telephone Number: (071) 736-6561
Car Parking: Street Parking
Coach Parking: Stevenage Road
Nearest Railway Station: Putney
Nearest Tube Station: Putney Bridge (District)
Club Shop:
Opening Times: Home Matchdays, Monday, Wednesday & Friday afternoons 2.00-4.00pm
Telephone No.: (071) 736-6561
Postal Sales: Yes
Nearest Police Station: Heckfield Place, Fulham
Police Force: Metropolitan
Police Telephone No.: (071) 385-1212

GROUND INFORMATION

Away Supporters' Entrances: Putney End
Away Supporters' Sections: Putney Terrace (Open)
Family Facilities: **Location of Stand**: Stevenage Road Stand ('B' Block)
Capacity of Stand: 377
Away Families: Accommodated in Family Stand

ADMISSION INFO (1993/94 PRICES)

Adult Standing: £6.50
Adult Seating: £10.00
Child Standing: £2.50
Child Seating: £4.00
Programme Price: £1.30
FAX Number: (071) 731-7047

STEVENAGE ROAD STAND (COTTAGE)

HAMMERSMITH END

PUTNEY END (Away)

RIVERSIDE STAND
River Thames

Travelling Supporters Information:
Routes: From North: Take A1/M1 to North Circular (A406) West to Neasden and follow signs Harlesdon A404, then Hammersmith A219. At Broadway follow Fulham sign and turn right (1 mile) into Harbord Street left at end to Ground; From South & East: Take South Circular (A205) and follow Putney Bridge sign (A219), Cross Bridge and follow Hammersmith signs for 0.5 mile, left into Bishops Park Road, then right at end; From West: Take M4 to A4 then branch left (2 miles) into Hammersmith Broadway (then as North).
Bus Services: Services 74 & 220 from tube station to Ground.

GILLINGHAM FC

Founded: 1893
Turned Professional: 1894
Limited Company: 1893
Admitted to League: 1920
Former Name(s): New Brompton FC
1893-1913
Nickname: 'Gills'
Ground: Priestfield Stadium, Redfern Avenue, Gillingham, Kent ME7 4DD

Record Attendance: 23,002 (10/1/48)
Colours: Shirts - Blue
Shorts - White
Telephone No.: (0634) 851854/851462
Ticket Information: (0634) 576828
Pitch Size: 114 × 75yds
Ground Capacity: 10,422
Seating Capacity: 1,225

GENERAL INFORMATION

Supporters Club Administrator:
Peter Lloyd
Address: c/o Club
Telephone Number: (0634) 851854
Car Parking: Street Parking
Coach Parking: By Police Direction
Nearest Railway Station: Gillingham
Nearest Bus Station: Gillingham
Club Shop:
Opening Times: Weekdays & Matchdays
10.00am-5.00pm
Telephone No.: (0634) 851462
Postal Sales: Yes
Nearest Police Station: Gillingham
Police Force: Kent
Police Telephone No.: (0634) 834488

GROUND INFORMATION

Away Supporters' Entrances: Redfern Avenue
Turnstiles
Away Supporters' Sections: Redfern Avenue Corner
(Gillingham End)
Family Facilities: **Location of Stand**:
Main Stand (Rainham End)
Capacity of Stand: 1,090

ADMISSION INFO (1994/95 PRICES)

Adult Standing: £6.50
Adult Seating: £8.50 - £10.00
Child Standing: £4.00
Child Seating: £6.00 - £10.00
Programme Price: £1.20
FAX Number: (0634) 850986

GORDON ROAD STAND

TORONTO ROAD
RAINHAM END

GILLINGHAM END
Priestfield Road

MAIN STAND
Redfern Avenue

Travelling Supporters Information:
Routes: From All Parts: Exit M2 junction 4 and follow link road (dual carriageway) B278 to 3rd roundabout. Turn left on to A2 (dual carriageway) across roundabout to traffic lights. Turn right Woodlands Road - after traffic lights. Ground 0.25 mile on left.

GRIMSBY TOWN FC

Founded: 1878
Turned Professional: 1890
Limited Company: 1890
Admitted to League: 1892
Former Name(s): Grimsby Pelham FC (1879)
Nickname: 'Mariners'
Ground: Blundell Park, Cleethorpes
DN35 7PY

Record Attendance: 31,651 (20/2/37)
Colours: Shirts - Black & White Stripes
Shorts - Black
Telephone No.: (0472) 697111
Ticket Information: (0472) 697111
Pitch Size: 111 × 74yds
Ground Capacity: 15,000 (Approximately)
Seating Capacity: 5,021

GENERAL INFORMATION

Supporters Club Administrator:
Rachel Branson
Address: 26 Humberstone Road, Grimsby
Telephone Number: (0472) 360050
Car Parking: Street Parking
Coach Parking: Harrington Street -
Near Ground
Nearest Railway Station: Cleethorpes (1.5
miles), New Clee (0.5 mile - specials only)
Nearest Bus Station: Brighowgate, Grimsby
(4 miles)
Club Shop: At ground (Shop Hours)
Opening Times: Monday-Friday 9.00-5.00
Match Saturdays 10.00-Kick-off
Telephone No.: (0472) 697111
Postal Sales: Yes
Nearest Police Station: Cleethorpes (Near
Railway Station) 1.5 miles
Police Force: Humberside
Police Telephone No.: (0472) 359171

GROUND INFORMATION

Away Supporters' Entrances: Harrington Street
Turnstiles 15-18, Constitutional Ave. Turnstiles 5-14
Away Supporters' Sections: Osmond Stand - Covered
standing and seats
Family Facilities: **Location of Stand**:
Main Stand (with access to family lounge)
Capacity of Stand: 120

ADMISSION INFO (1994/95 PRICES)

Adult Standing: £8.00   (Away fans £8.00)
Adult Seating: £11.00 - £12.00   (Away fans £12.00)
Child Standing: £4.00   (No concessions for
Child Seating: £5.00   Away fans)
Programme Price: £1.30
FAX Number: (0472) 693665
N.B. Special Family Rate in Main Stand

(CLEETHORPES) Grimsby Road   To Grimsby
FINDUS STAND

Neville Street
OSMOND STAND
(Away)

Blundell Avenue
PONTOON STAND

MAIN STAND
Harrington Street

Travelling Supporters Information:

Routes: From All Parts except Lincolnshire and East Anglia: Take M180 to A180 follow signs to Grimsby/
Cleethorpes. A180 ends at roundabout (3rd in short distance after crossing Docks), take 2nd exit from roundabout over Railway flyover into Cleethorpes Road (A1098) and continue into Grimsby Road. After second
stretch of Dual Carriageway, Ground 0.5 mile on left; From Lincolnshire: Take A46 or A16 and follow
Cleethorpes signs along (A1098) Weelsby Road (2 miles) and take 1st exit at roundabout at end of Clee Road
into Grimsby Road. Ground 1.75 miles on right.

HARTLEPOOL UNITED FC

Founded: 1908
Turned Professional: 1908
Limited Company: 1908
Admitted to League: 1921
Former Name(s): Hartlepools United FC
(1908-68); Hartlepool FC (1968-77)
Nickname: 'The Pool'
Ground: Victoria Ground, Clarence Road,
Hartlepool TS24 8BZ

Record Attendance: 17,426 (15/1/57)
Colours: Shirts - Blue & Sky Blue
Shorts - Blue & Sky Blue
Telephone No.: (0429) 272584
Ticket Information: (0429) 222077
Pitch Size: 113 × 77yds
Ground Capacity: 6,721
Seating Capacity: 2,800 (During 1994/95)

GENERAL INFORMATION
Supporters Club Administrator:
D. Lattimer
Address: 4 Friarage Gardens, Hartlepool
Telephone Number: -
Car Parking: Street Parking
Coach Parking: Church Street
Nearest Railway Station: Hartlepool Church
Street (5 minutes walk)
Nearest Bus Station: Church Street
Club Shop:
Opening Times: Weekdays 9.00-5.00
Saturdays 9.00-2.30
Telephone No.: (0429) 222077
Postal Sales: Yes
Nearest Police Station: Avenue Road,
Hartlepool
Police Force: Cleveland
Police Telephone No.: (0429) 221151

GROUND INFORMATION
Away Supporters' Entrances: Clarence Road
Turnstiles 1, 2 & 3
Away Supporters' Sections: Town End, Clarence Rd.
Family Facilities: Location of Stand:
Family Enclosure - Millhouse Stand
Capacity of Stand: -

ADMISSION INFO (1994/95 PRICES)
Adult Standing: £6.00
Adult Seating: £8.00
Child Standing: £4.00
Child Seating: £5.00
Programme Price: £1.20
FAX Number: (0429) 863007

BUS

CLARENCE ROAD

RINK END

TOWN END (Away)

MILLHOUSE STAND
RABY ROAD

Travelling Supporters Information:
Routes: From North: Take A1/A19 then A179 towards Hartlepool to Hart. Straight across traffic lights (2.5 miles) to cross-roads, then turn left into Clarence Road; From South & West: Take A1/A19 or A689 into Town Centre then bear left into Clarence Road.

HEREFORD UNITED FC

Founded: 1924
Turned Professional: 1924
Limited Company: 1939
Admitted to League: 1972
Former Name(s): None
Nickname: 'United'
Ground: Edgar Street, Hereford   HR4 9JU

Record Attendance: 18,114 (4/1/58)
Colours: Shirts - White
            Shorts - Black
Telephone No.: (0432) 276666
Ticket Information: (0432) 276666
Pitch Size: 111 × 74yds
Ground Capacity: 13,752
Seating Capacity: 2,897

GENERAL INFORMATION
Supporters Club Administrator:
K. Benjimen
Address: c/o Club
Telephone Number: (0432) 265005
Car Parking: Merton Meadow & Edgar Street Car Parks
Coach Parking: Cattle Market (Near Ground)
Nearest Railway Station: Hereford (0.5 mile)
Nearest Bus Station: Commercial Road, Hereford
Club Shop:
Opening Times: Matchdays & Weekdays via Commercial Office
Telephone No.: (0432) 276666
Postal Sales: Yes
Nearest Police Station: Bath Street, Hereford
Police Force: Hereford
Police Telephone No.: (0432) 276422

GROUND INFORMATION
Away Supporters' Entrances: Blackfriars Street and Edgar Street
Away Supporters' Sections: Blackfriars Street End
Family Facilities: **Location of Stand**:
Edgar Street Side
Capacity of Stand: 300

ADMISSION INFO (1994/95 PRICES)
Adult Standing: £5.00
Adult Seating: £7.00
Child Standing: £4.00
Child Seating: £5.00
Programme Price: £1.00
FAX Number: (0432) 341359

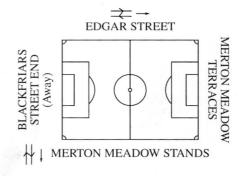

EDGAR STREET

BLACKFRIARS STREET END (Away)

MERTON MEADOW TERRACES

MERTON MEADOW STANDS

Travelling Supporters Information:
Routes: From North: Follow A49 Hereford signs straight into Edgar Street; From East: Take A465 or A438 into Hereford Town Centre, then follow signs for Leominster (A49) into Edgar Street; From South: Take A49 or A465 into Town Centre (then as East); From West: Take A438 into Town Centre (then as East).

HUDDERSFIELD TOWN FC

Founded: 1908
Turned Professional: 1908
Limited Company: 1908
Admitted to League: 1910
Former Name(s): None
Nickname: 'Terriers'
Ground: The Kirklees Stadium, Leeds Road, Huddersfield HD1 6PX

Record Attendance: 67,037 (27/2/32)
Colours: Shirts - Blue & White Stripes
Shorts - Blue
Telephone No.: (0484) 420335
Ticket Information: (0484) 424444
Pitch Size: 115 × 75yds
Ground Capacity: 20,300
Seating Capacity: 20,300

GENERAL INFORMATION
Supporters Club Administrator:
Mrs M. Procter
Address: 23 Lincroft Avenue, Dalton, Huddersfield, HD5 8DS
Telephone Number: (0484) 532465
Car Parking: Car Park for 1,100 cars adjacent
Coach Parking: Adjacent Car Park
Nearest Railway Station: Huddersfield (1.25 miles)
Nearest Bus Station: Huddersfield
Club Shop:
Opening Times: Weekdays 9.00am-7.30pm & Saturdays 9.00am-3.00pm
Telephone No.: (0484) 534867
Postal Sales: Yes
Nearest Police Station: Huddersfield (1 mile)
Police Force: West Yorkshire
Police Telephone No.: (0484) 422122

GROUND INFORMATION
Away Supporters' Entrances: South Stand
Away Supporters' Sections: South Stand
Family Facilities: **Location of Stand**:
Riverside Stand, Lower Tier
Capacity of Stand: 5,100

ADMISSION INFO (1994/95 PRICES)
Adult Seating: £7.50
Child Seating: £4.00
Programme Price: £1.20
FAX Number: (0484) 515122

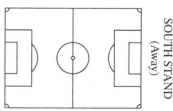

KILNER BANK STAND

SOUTH STAND (Away)

RIVERSIDE STAND

Travelling Supporters Information:
Routes: From North, East & West: Exit M62 junction 25 and take the A644 and A62 following Huddersfield signs. Follow signs for Kirklees Stadium. From South: Leave M1 at Junction 38 then follow A637/A642 to Huddersfield. At Ring Road follow signs A62 Kirklees Stadium.
Bus Services: Services 220, 221, 201/2/3

HULL CITY FC

Founded: 1904
Turned Professional: 1904
Limited Company: 1904
Admitted to League: 1905
Former Name(s): None
Nickname: 'Tigers'
Ground: Boothferry Park, Boothferry Road, Hull HU4 6EU

Record Attendance: 55,019 (26/2/49)
Colours: Shirts - Black & Amber
Shorts - Black
Telephone No.: (0482) 51119
Ticket Information: (0482) 51119
Pitch Size: 115 × 75yds
Ground Capacity: 17,208
Seating Capacity: 5,495

GENERAL INFORMATION
Supporters Club Administrator:
F. Anholm
Address: c/o Club
Telephone Number: (0482) 632987
Car Parking: Limited Parking at Ground
Street Parking
Coach Parking: At Ground
Nearest Railway Station: Hull Paragon
(1.5 miles)
Nearest Bus Station: Ferensway, Hull
(1.5 miles)
Club Shop: Paragon Square, Hull & at
Ground
Opening Times: Weekdays 9.30-4.30
Matchdays 10.00-3.00 - Ground
Telephone No.: (0482) 51119/28297
Postal Sales: Yes
Nearest Police Station: Central, Hull
(2 miles)
Police Force: Humberside
Police Telephone No.: (0482) 210031

GROUND INFORMATION
Away Supporters' Entrances: North Stand Turnstiles
Away Supporters' Sections: Visitor's enclosure,
North Stand plus seating area in West Stand
Family Facilities: Location of Stand:
Main Stand
Capacity of Stand: 568

ADMISSION INFO (1994/95 PRICES)
Adult Standing: £7.00
Adult Seating: £8.00 - £10.00
Child Standing: £3.00
Child Seating: £4.00 - £5.00
Programme Price: £1.20
FAX Number: (0482) 565752

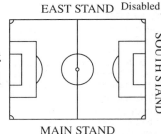

Travelling Supporters Information:
Routes: From North: Take A1 or A19 then A1079 into City Centre and follow signs for Leeds (A63) into Anlaby Road. At roundabout (1 mile) take 1st exit into Boothferry Road; From West: Take M62 to A63 to Hull. Fork left after Ferriby Crest Motel to Humber Bridge roundabout, then take 1st exit to Boothferry Road (Ground 1.5 miles). Do NOT follow Clive Sullivan way; From South: Non-scenic alternative route take M18 to M62 (then as West). Or use motorways M1 to M18 then M180 and follow signs over Humber Bridge (Toll), take 2nd exit at roundabout (A63) towards Boothferry Road (Ground 1.5 miles).

IPSWICH TOWN FC

Founded: 1887	**Record Attendance**: 38,010 (8/3/75)
Turned Professional: 1936	**Colours**: Shirts - Blue with White Sleeves
Limited Company: 1936	Shorts - White
Admitted to League: 1938	**Telephone No.**: (0473) 219211
Former Name(s): None	**Ticket Information**: (0473) 221133
Nickname: 'Town' 'Super Blues'	**Pitch Size**: 112 × 70yds
Ground: Portman Road, Ipswich IP1 2DA	**Ground Capacity**: 22,559
	Seating Capacity: 22,559

GENERAL INFORMATION
Supporters Club Administrator:
Mr. G. Dodson
Address: c/o Club
Telephone Number: (0473) 219211
Car Parking: Portman Road and Portman Walk Car Parks
Coach Parking: Portman Walk
Nearest Railway Station: Ipswich (5 mins)
Nearest Bus Station: Ipswich
Club Shop:
Opening Times: Weekdays & Matchdays 9.00-5.00
Telephone No.: (0473) 214614
Postal Sales: Yes
Nearest Police Station: Civic Drive, Ipswich (5 minutes walk)
Police Force: Suffolk
Police Telephone No.: (0473) 55811

GROUND INFORMATION
Away Supporters' Entrances: Portman Road Turnstiles C & D
Away Supporters' Sections: Portman Road C & D
Family Facilities: Location of Stand:
South side of Pioneer Stand & Portman Lower Terrace
Capacity of Stands: Approximately 3,000

ADMISSION INFO (1994/95 PRICES)
Adult Seating: £8.50 - £16.00
Child Seating: £5.00 - £16.00
Programme Price: £1.50
FAX Number: (0473) 226835

PORTMAN ROAD (Away)
PORTMAN STAND

PORTMAN WALK NORTH STAND

CHURCHMAN'S END SOUTH STAND

PIONEER STAND
CONSTANTINE ROAD

Travelling Supporters Information:
Routes: From North & West: Take A45 following signs for Ipswich West only. Proceed through Post House traffic lights and at 2nd set of traffic lights turn right into West End Road, ground 0.25 mile along on left; From South: Follow signs for Ipswich West then as North and West.

LEEDS UNITED FC

Founded: 1919	**Record Attendance**: 57,892 (15/3/67)
Turned Professional: 1919	**Colours**: Shirts - White
Limited Company: 1919	Shorts - White
Admitted to League: 1920	**Telephone No.**: (0532) 716037
Former Name(s): Formed after Leeds City FC	**Ticket Information**: (0532) 710710
wound up for 'Irregular Practices'	**Pitch Size**: 117 × 76yds
Nickname: 'United'	**Ground Capacity**: 38,500 Approximately
Ground: Elland Road, Leeds LS11 0ES	**Seating Capacity**: 38,500 Approximately

GENERAL INFORMATION
Supporters Club Administrator:
Eric Carlile
Address: c/o Club
Telephone Number: (0532) 716037
Car Parking: Large Car Parks (Adjacent)
Coach Parking: By Police Direction
Nearest Railway Station: Leeds City
Nearest Bus Station: Leeds City Centre -
Specials from Swinegate
Club Shop:
Opening Times: Weekdays 9.15-5.00,
Matchdays 9.15-Kick-off
Telephone No.: (0532) 706844
Postal Sales: Yes (send SAE)
Nearest Police Station: Holbeck, Leeds
(3 miles)
Police Force: West Yorkshire
Police Telephone No.: (0532) 435353

GROUND INFORMATION
Away Supporters' Entrances: South East Corner
Away Supporters' Sections: South East Corner
Family Facilities: **Location of Stand**:
East Stand
Capacity of Stand: 10,000

ADMISSION INFO (1994/95 PRICES)
Adult Seating: £13.00 - £19.00
Child Seating: Half-price for Members only
Programme Price: £1.50
FAX Number: (0532) 706560

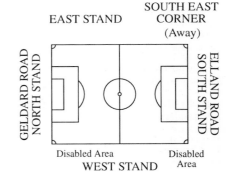

Travelling Supporters Information:
Routes: From North: Take A58 or A61 into City Centre and follow signs to M621; Leave Motorway after 1.5 miles and exit roundabout on to A643 into Elland Road; From North-East: Take A63 or A64 into City Centre (then as North); From South: Take M1 to M621 (then as North); From West: Take M62 to M621 (then as North).

LEICESTER CITY FC

Founded: 1884
Turned Professional: 1894
Limited Company: 1894
Admitted to League: 1894
Former Name(s): Leicester Fosse FC
(1884-1919)
Nickname: 'Filberts' 'Foxes'
Ground: City Stadium, Filbert Street,
Leicester LE2 7FL

Record Attendance: 47,298 (18/2/28)
Colours: Shirts - Blue with White Collars
Shorts - White
Telephone No.: (0533) 555000
Ticket Information: (0533) 555000
Pitch Size: 112 × 75yds
Ground Capacity: 23,500
Seating Capacity: 23,500

GENERAL INFORMATION

Supporters Club Administrator:
C. Ginetta
Address: c/o Club
Telephone Number: (0533) 555000
Car Parking: NCP Car Park (5 mins. walk)
& Street Parking
Coach Parking: Western Boulevard
Nearest Railway Station: Leicester (1 mile)
Nearest Bus Station: St.Margaret's (1 mile)
Club Shop:
Opening Times: Weekdays 9.00-5.00
(closes for lunch), Matchdays 10.00-3.00
Telephone No.: (0533) 555000
Postal Sales: Yes
Nearest Police Station: Charles Street,
Leicester
Police Force: Leicester
Police Telephone No.: (0533) 530066

GROUND INFORMATION

Away Supporters' Entrances: East Stand, Block T
Turnstiles
Away Supporters' Sections: Spion Kop enclosure
(covered)/Block T East Stand
Family Facilities: Location of Stand:
By Member's Stand
Capacity of Stand: 2,600

ADMISSION INFO (1994/95 PRICES)

Adult Seating: £10.00 - £17.00
Child Seating: £5.00 - £9.00
Programme Price: £1.20
FAX Number: (0533) 470585

Travelling Supporters Information:
Routes: From North: Take A46/A607 into City Centre or exit M1 junction 22 for City Centre, follow
'Rugby' signs into Almond Road, turn right at end into Aylestone Road, turn left into Walnut Street and left
again into Filbert Street; From East: Take A47 into City Centre (then as for North); From South: Exit M1
junction 21 and take A46, turn right 0.75 mile after Railway bridge into Upperton Road, then right into Filbert
Street; From West: Take M69 to City Centre (then as North).

LEYTON ORIENT FC

GENERAL INFORMATION
Supporters Club Administrator: D.Dodd
Address: c/o Club
Telephone Number: (081) 539-6156
Car Parking: NCP Brisbane Road & Street Parking
Coach Parking: By Police Direction
Nearest Railway Station: Leyton Midland Road (0.5 mile)
Nearest Tube Station: Leyton (Central)
Club Shop:
Opening Times: Monday-Friday (Wednesday closed) 10.00-4.30pm
Telephone No.: (081) 539-2223
Postal Sales: Yes
Nearest Police Station: Francis Road, Leyton, London   E10
Police Force: Metropolitan
Police Telephone No.: (081) 556-8855

GROUND INFORMATION
Away Supporters' Entrances: South Terrace Turnstiles
Away Supporters' Sections: South Terrace (Open)
Family Facilities: Location of Stand: North Wing
Capacity of Stand: not specified

ADMISSION INFO (1994/95 PRICES)
Adult Standing: £7.00
Adult Seating: £8.00, £9.00 or £11.00
Child Standing: £3.50
Child Seating: £4.00 or £6.00
Programme Price: £1.20
FAX Number: (081) 539-4390

```
                    OLIVER ROAD
                    WEST STAND
  BUCKINGHAM ROAD
  SOUTH TERRACE (Away)                    WINDSOR ROAD
                                          NORTH TERRACE

                    MAIN STAND
                    BRISBANE ROAD
```

Travelling Supporters Information:
Routes: From North & West: Take A406 North Circular and follow signs Chelmsford, to Edmonton, after 2.5 miles 3rd exit at roundabout towards Leyton (A112). Pass railway station and turn right (0.5 mile) into Windsor Road and left into Brisbane Road; From East: Follow A12 to London then City for Leytonstone follow Hackney signs into Grove Road, cross Main Road into Ruckholt Road and turn right into Leyton High Road, turn left (0.25 mile) into Buckingham Road, then left into Brisbane Road; From South: Take A102M through Blackwall Tunnel and follow signs to Newmarket (A102) to join A11 to Stratford, then signs Stratford Station into Leyton Road to railway station (then as North).

LINCOLN CITY FC

Founded: 1883
Turned Professional: 1892
Limited Company: 1892
Admitted to League: 1892
Former Name(s): None
Nickname: 'Red Imps'
Ground: Sincil Bank, Lincoln   LN5 8LD

Record Attendance: 23,196 (15/11/67)
Colours: Shirts - Red & White Stripes
Shorts - Black
Telephone No.: (0522) 522224
Ticket Information: (0522) 522224
Pitch Size: 110 × 76yds
Ground Capacity: 5,186
Seating Capacity: 3,524

GENERAL INFORMATION
Supporters Club Administrator: -
Address: c/o Club
Telephone Number: (0522) 522224
Car Parking: Adjacent to Ground (£2.00)
Coach Parking: South Common (300 yards)
Nearest Railway Station: Lincoln Central
Nearest Tube Station: Lincoln Central
Club Shop: At Ground, St. Andrews Stand
Opening Times: Weekdays & Matchdays
9.00-5.00
Telephone No.: (0522) 522224
Postal Sales: Yes
Nearest Police Station: West Parade, Lincoln
(1.5 miles)
Police Force: Lincolnshire
Police Telephone No.: (0522) 529911

GROUND INFORMATION
Away Supporters' Entrances: South Park Stand
Away Supporters' Sections: South Park Stand - (Seating only)
Family Facilities: **Location of Stand**:
St. Andrew's Stand & E.G.T. Family Stand
Capacity of Stand: 650

ADMISSION INFO (1993/94 PRICES)
Adult Standing: £5.00 - £5.50
Adult Seating: £5.50 - £7.50
Child Standing: £3.50
Child Seating: £4.50 - £5.50
Programme Price: £1.00
FAX Number: (0522) 520564
Away Seating: £6.00
Various concessions available in Family Sections

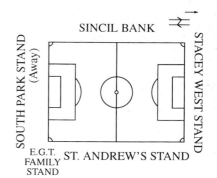

Travelling Supporters Information:
Routes: From East: Take A46 or A158 into City Centre following Newark (A46) signs into High Street. Pass under railway bridge and take next left (Scorer Street & Cross Street) for Ground; From North & West: Take A15 or A57 into City Centre then as East; From South: Take A1 to A46 for City Centre then into High Street and turn right into Scorer Street, then right again into Cross Street for Ground.

LIVERPOOL FC

Founded: 1892
Turned Professional: 1892
Limited Company: 1892
Admitted to League: 1893
Former Name(s): None
Nickname: 'Reds'
Ground: Anfield Road, Liverpool   L4 0TH
Record Attendance: 61,905 (2/2/52)

Colours: Shirts - Red with White Markings
Shorts - Red with White Markings
Telephone No.: (051) 263-2361
Ticket Information: (051) 260-8680
Credit Card Bookings: (051) 263-5727
Pitch Size: 110 × 75yds
Ground Capacity: 41,000 Approximately
Seating Capacity: 41,000

GENERAL INFORMATION
Supporters Club Administrator: -
Address: Liverpool International Supporters Club, c/o Club
Telephone Number: (051) 263-2361
Car Parking: Stanley Park car park (adjacent)
Coach Parking: Priory Rd. & Pinehurst Ave.
Nearest Railway Station: Kirkdale
Nearest Bus Station: Skelhorne Street, Liverpool
Club Shop:
Opening Times: Monday-Saturday 9.30-5.30
Telephone No.: (051) 263-1760
Postal Sales: Yes
Nearest Police Station: Walton Lane, Liverpool (1.5 miles)
Police Force: Merseyside
Police Telephone No.: (051) 709-6010

Note: The new Spion Kop Grandstand is expected to be completed by January 1995.

GROUND INFORMATION
Away Supporters' Entrances: Anfield Road
Away Supporters' Sections: Visitors Section, Anfield Road (Covered)
Family Facilities: **Location of Stand**: Anfield Road End
Capacity of Stand: 1,300

ADMISSION INFO (1993/94 PRICES)
Adult Seating: Grade 'A' games £14   Grade 'B' £13
Child Seating: Grade 'A' games £5   Grade 'B' £4.50
Programme Price: £1.20
FAX Number: (051) 260-8813
Ticket Office FAX: (051) 261-1416
Note : Prices vary depending on opponents

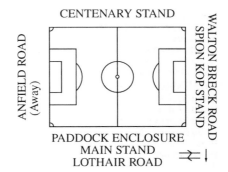

Travelling Supporters Information:
Routes: From North: Exit M6 junction 28 and follow Liverpool A58 signs into Walton Hall Avenue, pass Stanley Park and turn left into Anfield Road; From South & East: Take M62 to end of motorway then turn right into Queen's Drive (A5058) and turn left (3 miles) into Utting Avenue, after 1 mile turn right into Anfield Road; From North Wales: Take Mersey Tunnel into City Centre and follow signs to Preston (A580) into Walton Hall Avenue, turn right into Anfield Road before Stanley Park.

LUTON TOWN FC

Founded: 1885
Turned Professional: 1890
Limited Company: 1897
Admitted to League: 1897
Former Name(s): Formed by amalgamation of Wanderers FC & Excelsior FC
Nickname: 'Hatters'
Ground: Kenilworth Road Stadium, 1 Maple Road, Luton   LU4 8AW

Record Attendance: 30,069 (4/3/59)
Colours: Shirts - White/Royal Blue/Orange
Shorts - Blue/Orange/White Trim
Telephone No.: (0582) 411622
Ticket Information: (0582) 30748
Pitch Size: 110 × 72yds
Ground Capacity: 10,499
Seating Capacity: 10,499

GENERAL INFORMATION
Supporters Club Administrator: Mrs.P.Gray
Address: 19 Kingsdown Avenue, Luton, Beds
Telephone Number: (0582) 391574
Car Parking: Street Parking
Coach Parking: Luton Bus Station
Nearest Railway Station: Luton (1 mile)
Nearest Bus Station: Bute Street, Luton
Club Shop: Kenilworth Road Forecourt
Opening Times: 9.00-5.00
Telephone No.: (0582) 411622
Postal Sales: Yes
Nearest Police Station:Buxton Road, Luton (0.75 mile)
Police Force: Bedfordshire
Police Telephone No.: (0582) 401212

GROUND INFORMATION
Away Supporters' Entrances: Oak Road
Away Supporters' Sections: Oak Stand
Family Facilities: Location of Stand: Kenilworth Stand
Capacity of Stand: 2,900

ADMISSION INFO (1994/95 PRICES)
Adult Seating: £7.00 - £14.50
Child Seating: £4.50 - £7.50
Programme Price: £1.50
FAX Number: (0582) 405070
Note : Lower prices apply when tickets are purchased at least 14 days before the game.

Travelling Supporters Information:
Routes: From North & West: Exit M1 junction 11 and follow signs to Luton (A505) into Dunstable Road. Follow one-way system and turn right back towards Dunstable, take first left into Oak Road; From South & East: Exit M1 junction 10 (or A6/A612) into Luton Town Centre and follow signs into Dunstable Road. After railway bridge take sixth turning on left into Oak Road.

MANCHESTER CITY FC

Founded: 1887
Turned Professional: 1887
Limited Company: 1894
Admitted to League: 1892
Former Name(s): Ardwick FC (1887-94)
Nickname: 'Citizens' 'City' 'Blues'
Ground: Maine Road, Moss Side,
Manchester M14 7WN

Record Attendance: 84,569 (3/3/34)
Colours: Shirts - Sky Blue
Shorts - White
Telephone No.: (061) 226-1191
Ticket Information: (061) 226-2224
Pitch Size: 117 × 76yds
Ground Capacity: 21,500 (Start of 1994/95)
Seating Capacity: 21,500

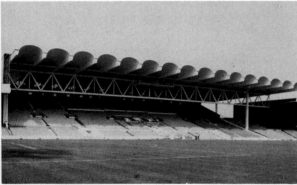

GENERAL INFORMATION
Supporters Club Administrator:
Frank Horrocks
Address: Manchester City Supporter's Club,
Maine Road, Manchester M14 7WN
Telephone Number: (061) 226-5047
Car Parking: Street Parking and Local
Schools
Coach Parking: Kippax Street Car Park
Nearest Railway Station: Manchester
Piccadilly (2.5 miles)
Nearest Bus Station: Chorlton Street
Club Shop:
Opening Times: Weekdays 9.30-5.00
Matchdays 9.30-5.30
Telephone No.: (061) 226-4824
Postal Sales: Yes
Nearest Police Station: Platt Lane,
Moss Side, Manchester
Police Force: Greater Manchester
Police Telephone No.: (061) 872-5050

GROUND INFORMATION
Away Supporters' Entrances: No facilities for Away
Supporters during Reconstruction of Ground
Away Supporters' Sections: No facilities
Family Facilities: Location of Stand:
Umbro Stand
Capacity of Stand: Not specified

ADMISSION INFO (1993/94 PRICES)
Adult Seating: £10.00, £11.00 or £12.00
Child Seating: £5.00 (Family Stand)
Programme Price: £1.40
FAX Number: (061) 227-9418

KIPPAX STREET STAND
(UNDER RECONSTRUCTION)

(CLAREMONT ROAD)
NORTH STAND

UMBRO STAND

MAIN STAND
(MAINE ROAD)

Travelling Supporters Information:
Routes: From North & West: Take M61 & M63 exit junction 9 following signs to Manchester (A5103).
Turn right at crossroads (2.75 miles) into Claremont Road. After 0.25 mile turn right into Maine Road; From
South: Exit M6 junction 19 to A556 and M56 junction 3 following signs to Manchester (A1503) (then as
North); From East: Exit M62 onto the M602 Salford Motorway. Follow this to its end and then take the right
hand lane and continue into Manchester along the A57. Pass Sainsburys and go under Railway Bridge head-
ing for the Mancunian Way. After 2 roundabouts join Mancunian Way (elevated road) but leave at first exit
and go under elevated section to roundabout then straight across. Follow road along past Dental Hospital into
Lloyd Street and continue along to the ground.

MANCHESTER UNITED FC

Founded: 1878
Turned Professional: 1902
Limited Company: 1907
Admitted to League: 1892
Former Name(s): Newton Heath LYR FC
(1878-1892); Newton Heath FC (1892-1902)
Nickname: 'Red Devils'
Ground: Old Trafford, Manchester M16 0RA

Record Attendance: 76,962 (25/3/39)
Colours: Shirts - Red
Shorts - White
Telephone No.: (061) 872-1661
Ticket Information: (061) 872-0199
Pitch Size: 116 × 76yds
Ground Capacity: 43,500
Seating Capacity: 43,500

GENERAL INFORMATION
Supporters Club Administrator:
Barry Moorhouse
Address: c/o Club
Telephone Number: (061) 872-5208
Car Parking: Lancashire Cricket Ground
(1,200 cars)
Coach Parking: By Police Direction
Nearest Railway Station: At Ground
Nearest Bus Station: Chorlton Street
Nearest Metro Station: Old Trafford
Club Shop:
- **Opening Times**: Weekdays 9.30-5.00pm;
Matchdays 9.30-3.00pm; Sundays 10.00-
4.00pm; Non-Match Saturdays 9.30-4.00pm
Telephone No.: (061) 872-3398
Postal Sales: Yes
Nearest Police Station: Talbot Road,
Stretford (0.5 mile)
Police Force: Greater Manchester
Police Telephone No.: (061) 872-5050

GROUND INFORMATION
Away Supporters' Entrances: Stand L
Away Supporters' Sections: Stand L
Family Facilities: Location of Stand:
South Stand & Stretford End
Capacity of Stand: 4,100

ADMISSION INFO (1994/95 PRICES)
Adult Seating: £10.00 - £16.00
Child Seating: £5.00 - £6.00
Programme Price: £1.50
FAX Number: (061) 896-5502

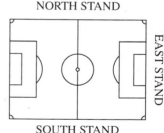

NORTH STAND

WEST STAND
STRETFORD END

EAST STAND

SOUTH STAND

Travelling Supporters Information:
Routes: From North & West: Take M61 to M63 and exit junction 4 and follow Manchester signs (A5081).
Turn right (2.5 miles) into Warwick Road; From South: Exit M6 junction 19 take Stockport (A556) then
Altrincham (A56). From Altrincham follow Manchester signs. turn left into Warwick Road (6 miles); From
East: Exit M62 junction 17 then A56 to Manchester. Follow signs South then Chester (Chester Road), turn
right into Warwick Road (2 miles).

MANSFIELD TOWN FC

Founded: 1891	**Record Attendance**: 24,467 (10/1/53)
Turned Professional: 1910	**Colours**: Shirts - Amber with Blue Trim
Limited Company: 1910	Shorts - Blue with Amber Trim
Admitted to League: 1931	**Telephone No.**: (0623) 23567
Former Name(s): Mansfield Wesleyans FC	**Ticket Information**: (0623) 23567
(1891-1905)	**Pitch Size**: 115 × 70yds
Nickname: 'Stags'	**Ground Capacity**: 10,315
Ground: Field Mill Ground, Quarry Lane,	**Seating Capacity**: 3,448
Mansfield, Notts.	

GENERAL INFORMATION
Supporters Club Administrator:
Miss M.Brown
Address: 44 Portland Avenue, Annesley
Woodhouse, Nottinghamshire
Telephone Number: (0623) 754-1823
Car Parking: Large Car Park at Ground
Coach Parking: Adjacent
Nearest Railway Station: Mansfield Alfreton Parkway - 9 miles (no public transport)
Nearest Bus Station: Mansfield
Club Shop:
Opening Times: Weekdays & Matchdays
9.00-5.00
Telephone No.: (0623) 658070
Postal Sales: Yes
Nearest Police Station: Mansfield (0.25 mile)
Police Force: Nottinghamshire
Police Telephone No.: (0623) 22622

GROUND INFORMATION
Away Supporters' Entrances: Quarry Lane Turnstiles
Away Supporters' Sections: Quarry Lane End (Open)
Family Facilities: Location of Stand:
Chad Family Stand
Capacity of Stand: 1,130

ADMISSION INFO (1994/95 PRICES)
Adult Standing: £8.00
Adult Seating: £10.00 (£8.00 in Family Stand)
Child Standing: £3.00
Child Seating: £5.00 (£4.00 in Family Stand)
Programme Price: £1.00
FAX Number: (0623) 25014

CHAD FAMILY STAND
(Disabled)

NORTH STAND

QUARRY LANE
(Away)

WEST STAND

Travelling Supporters Information:
Routes: From North: Exit M1 junction 29, take A617 to Mansfield. After 6.25 miles turn right at Leisure Centre into Rosemary Street. Carry on to Quarry Lane and turn right; From South & West: Exit M1 junction 28, take A38 to Mansfield, after 6.5 miles turn right at crossroads into Belvedere Street, turn right after 0.25 mile into Quarry Lane; From East: Take A617 to Rainworth, turn left at crossroads (3 miles) into Windsor Road and turn right at end into Nottingham Road, then left into Quarry Lane.

MIDDLESBROUGH FC

Founded: 1876	**Record Attendance**: 53,596 (27/12/49)
Turned Professional: 1889	**Colours**: Shirts - Red with White Yoke
Limited Company: 1892	Shorts - White
Admitted to League: 1899	**Telephone No.**: (0642) 819659
Former Name(s): None	**Ticket Information**: (0642) 815996
Nickname: 'Boro'	**Pitch Size**: 114 × 73yds
Ground: Ayresome Park, Middlesbrough,	**Ground Capacity**: 26,101
Cleveland TS1 4PB	**Seating Capacity**: 12,585

GENERAL INFORMATION
Supporters Club Secretary:
Simon Bolton
Address: c/o Club
Telephone Number: (0642) 470512
Car Parking: Street Parking
Coach Parking: By Police Direction
Nearest Railway Station: Middlesbrough
(1 mile)
Nearest Bus Station: Middlesbrough
Club Shop:
Opening Times: Monday-Friday 9.30-5.00
+ Saturdays 10.00-12.00 + Matchdays
Telephone No.: (0642) 826664
Postal Sales: Yes
Nearest Police Station: Dunning Street,
Middlesbrough (1 mile)
Police Force: Cleveland
Police Telephone No.: (0642) 248184

GROUND INFORMATION
Away Supporters' Entrances: Turnstiles -South East
Corner
Away Supporters' Sections: South East Corner (Open
& Seating)
Family Facilities: **Location of Stand**:
East Stand & other locations
Capacity of Stand: 4,075

ADMISSION INFO (1994/95 PRICES)
Adult Standing: £8.00
Adult Seating: £8 - £12   (£6.00 in Family Group)
Child Standing: £3.00
Child Seating: £4.00
Programme Price: £1.00
FAX Number: (0642) 820244

Disabled
Section

AYRESOME STREET
NORTH STAND

WEST TERRACE
HOLGATE END

(AYRESOME PARK ROAD)
EAST STAND

SOUTH STAND
CLIVE ROAD

South-East
Corner (Away)

Travelling Supporters Information:
Routes: From North: Take A19 across Tees Bridge and join A66 (0.25 mile). Take Cannon Park exit then take 3rd exit at roundabout (0.5 mile) into Heywood Street, and left into Ayresome Street at end; From South: Take A1 & A19 to junction with A66, take 4th exit at roundabout (0.5 mile) into Heywood Street (then as North); From West: Take A66 then 1.5 miles after Teesside Park Racecourse take 4th exit at roundabout into Ayresome Street.

MILLWALL FC

GENERAL INFORMATION
Supporters Club Administrator: None
Address: -
Telephone Number: -
Car Parking: Juno Way
Coach Parking: Adjacent to Ground
Nearest Railway Station: New Cross Gate/ South Bermondsey (0.5 mile)
Nearest Tube Station: New Cross Gate/ Surrey Quays (0.5 mile)
Club Shop: Next to Stadium
Opening Times: Daily 9.30-4.30
Telephone No.: (071) 232-1222
Postal Sales: Yes
Nearest Police Station: Deptford/Lewisham (1 mile)
Police Force: Metropolitan
Police Telephone No.: (071) 679-9217

GROUND INFORMATION
Away Supporters' Entrances: North East Stand Turnstiles **31-36**
Away Supporters' Sections: North Stand
Family Facilities: **Location of Stand**: Upper Tier East Stand
Capacity of Stand: 800

ADMISSION INFO (1994/95 PRICES)
Adult Seating: £10.00 - £20.00
Child Seating: £4.50 - £10.00
Programme Price: £1.50
FAX Number: (071) 231-3663

WEST STAND

SOUTH STAND

NORTH STAND (Away)

EAST STAND

Travelling Supporters Information:
Routes: From North: Follow City signs from M1/A1 then signs for Shoreditch and Whitechapel. Follow signs Ring Road, Dover, cross over Tower Bridge, take 1st exit at roundabout (1 mile) onto A2. From Elephant & Castle take A2 (New Kent Road) into Old Kent Road and turn left (after 4 miles) at Canterbury Arms Pub into Ilderton Road then follow Surrey Canal Road to new ground in Zampa Road; From South: Take A20 and A21 following signs to London. At New Cross follow signs for stadium; From East: Take A2 to New Cross (then as South); From West: From M4 and M3 follow South Circular (A205) following signs for Clapham, City A3 then Camberwell, New Cross and then as South.

NEWCASTLE UNITED FC

Founded: 1882	**Record Attendance**: 68,386 (3/9/30)
Turned Professional: 1889	**Colours**: Shirts - Black and White Stripes
Limited Company: 1890	Shorts - Black
Admitted to League: 1893	**Telephone No.**: (091) 232-8361
Former Name(s): Newcastle East End FC	**Ticket Information**: (091) 261-1571
(1882-92) Became 'United' when amalgamated	**Pitch Size**: 115 × 75yds
with Newcastle West End FC	**Ground Capacity**: 32,536
Nickname: 'Magpies'	**Seating Capacity**: 32,536

Ground: St.James Park, Newcastle-Upon-Tyne NE1 4ST

GENERAL INFORMATION

Supporters Club Administrator: -
Address: -
Telephone Number: -
Car Parking: Street Parking
Coach Parking: By Police Direction
Nearest Railway Station: Newcastle Central (0.5 mile)
Nearest Bus Station: Gallowgate (0.25 mile)
Club Shop: At Ground, Eldon Square, Haymarket and MetroCentre
Opening Times: All shops are open Monday to Saturday 9.00-5.00. Eldon & Haymarket open until 8.00pm on Thursdays. MetroCentre open until at least 7.00pm Monday-Saturday.
Telephone No.: (091) 261-6357
Postal Sales: Yes
Phone: (091) 461-0000
Nearest Police Station: Market Street, Newcastle
Police Force: Northumbria
Police Telephone No.: (091) 232-3451

GROUND INFORMATION

Away Supporters' Entrances: North East Corner
Away Supporters' Sections: Sir John Hall Stand
Family Facilities: **Location of Stand**: East Stand Paddock
Capacity of Stand: 792 seated

ADMISSION INFO (1994/95 PRICES)

Adult Seating: £15.00
Child Seating: £12.50
Programme Price: £1.50
FAX Number: (091) 232-9875
Note: It is expected that only Season Ticket Holders will be admitted in 1994/95.

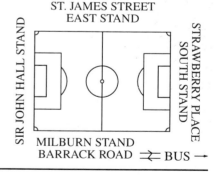

Travelling Supporters Information:

Routes: From North: Follow A1 into Newcastle, then Hexham signs into Percy Street. Turn right into Leazes Park Road; From South: Take A1M, then after Birtley Granada Services take A69 Gateshead Western Bypass (bear left on Motorway). Follow Airport signs for approximately 3 miles then take A692 (Newcastle) sign, crossing the Redheugh Bridge. At roundabout take 3rd exit (Blenheim Street). Proceed over two sets of traffic lights crossing Westmorland Road and Westgate Road. Turn left into Bath Lane. Over traffic lights to next roundabout and take third exit into Barrack Road; From West: Take A69 towards City Centre. Pass Newcastle General Hospital. At traffic lights immediately after Hospital turn left into Brighton Grove and after 70 yards turn right into Stanhope Street. Proceed into Barrack Road.

NORTHAMPTON TOWN FC

Founded: 1897
Turned Professional: 1901
Limited Company: 1901
Admitted to League: 1920
Former Name(s): None
Nickname: 'Cobblers'
Ground: Sixfields Stadium, Upton Way, Northampton

Record Attendance: -
Colours: Shirts - Claret
Shorts - White
Telephone No.: (0604) 234100
Ticket Information: (0604) 234100
Pitch Size: 112 × 75yds
Ground Capacity: 8,000
Seating Capacity: 8,000

GENERAL INFORMATION
Supporters Club Administrator:
Alec Smith
Address: c/o Club
Telephone Number: (0604) 842636
Car Parking: At Ground
Coach Parking: At Ground
Nearest Railway Station: Northampton Castle (1.25 miles)
Nearest Bus Station: Greyfriars
Club Shop:
Opening Times: Weekdays - 9.00-5.30pm
Matchdays 9.30-5.00
Telephone No.: (0604) 234100
Postal Sales: Yes
Nearest Police Station: Cambell Square, Northampton
Police Force: Northants
Police Telephone No.: (0604) 33221

GROUND INFORMATION
Away Supporters' Entrances: South Stand
Away Supporters' Sections: South & East Stands
Family Facilities: **Location of Stand**:
East Stand
Capacity of Stand: Not known

ADMISSION INFO (1994/95 PRICES)
Adult Seating: £7.00 to £10.00
Child Seating: £4.00 to £6.00
Programme Price: £1.20
FAX Number: (0604) 604176

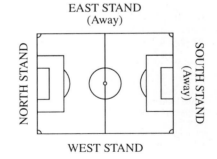

EAST STAND
(Away)

NORTH STAND

SOUTH STAND
(Away)

WEST STAND

Travelling Supporters Information:
Routes: From All Parts: Exit the M1 at junction 15A following the signs for the stadium onto Upton Way - the Ground is approximately 2 miles.

NORWICH CITY FC

Founded: 1902	**Record Attendance**: 43,984 (30/3/63)
Turned Professional: 1905	**Colours**: Shirts - Yellow
Limited Company: 1905	Shorts - Green
Admitted to League: 1920	**Telephone No.**: (0603) 760760
Former Name(s): None	**Ticket Information**: (0603) 761661
Nickname: 'Canaries'	**Pitch Size**: 114 × 74yds
Ground: Carrow Road, Norwich NR1 1JE	**Ground Capacity**: 21,272
	Seating Capacity: 21,272

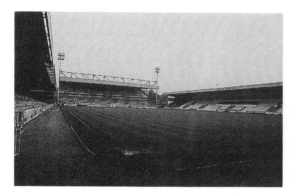

GENERAL INFORMATION

Supporters Club Administrator: Kevan Platt
Address: Club Canary, Carrow Road, Norwich
Telephone Number: (0603) 760760
Car Parking: City Centre Car Parks (nearby)
Coach Parking: Lower Clarence Road
Nearest Railway Station: Norwich Thorpe (1 mile)
Nearest Bus Station: Surrey Street, Norwich
Club Shop: (In City Stand)
Opening Times: Weekdays & Matchdays 9.00-4.45pm
Telephone No.: (0603) 761125
Postal Sales: Yes
Nearest Police Station: Bethel Street, Norwich (1 mile)
Police Force: Norfolk
Police Telephone No.: (0603) 768769

GROUND INFORMATION

Away Supporters' Entrances: Turnstiles 1-3
Away Supporters' Sections: South Stand - Blocks F & G (Covered)
Family Facilities: Location of Stand: South Stand
Capacity of Stand: 1,630

ADMISSION INFO (1993/94 PRICES)

Adult Seating: £8.00 - £19.00
Child Seating: £4.00 - £9.00
Programme Price: £1.50
FAX Number: (0603) 665510

SOUTH STAND (Disabled) (Away)
CARROW ROAD / BARCLAY STAND
RIVER END STAND
CITY STAND CARROW ROAD

Travelling Supporters Information:
Routes: From South: Take A11 or A140 and turn right onto A47 towards Great Yarmouth & Lowestoft, take A146 Norwich/Lowestoft sliproad, turn left towards Norwich and follow road signs for the Ground; From West: Take A47 on to A146 Norwich/Lowestoft slip road. Turn left towards Norwich, follow the road signs for the Ground.

NOTTINGHAM FOREST FC

Founded: 1865
Turned Professional: 1889
Limited Company: 1982
Admitted to League: 1892
Former Name(s): None
Nickname: 'Reds'   'Forest'
Ground: City Ground, Nottingham
NG2 5FJ

Record Attendance: 49,945 (28/10/67)
Colours: Shirts - Red
           Shorts - White
Telephone No.: (0602) 526000
Ticket Information: (0602) 526002
Pitch Size: 115 × 78yds
Ground Capacity: 22,300
Seating Capacity: 22,300

GENERAL INFORMATION
Supporters Club Administrator:
Mr. B. Tewson
Address: c/o Club
Telephone Number: (0602) 526000
Car Parking: East Car Park (300 cars) &
Street Parking
Coach Parking: East Car Park, Meadow Lane
Nearest Railway Station: Nottingham
Midland (0.5 mile)
Nearest Bus Station: Victoria Street/
Broadmarsh Centre
Club Shop:
Opening Times: Weekdays 9.00-5.00
Matchdays 9.00-3.00
Telephone No.: (0602) 826026
Postal Sales: Yes
Nearest Police Station: Rectory Road, West
Bridgford (1 mile)
Police Force: Nottinghamshire
Police Telephone No.: (0602) 481888

GROUND INFORMATION
Away Supporters' Entrances: Via East Car Park
Away Supporters' Sections: Bridgford Stand Lower
Tier
Family Facilities: **Location of Stand**:
Blocks G & Q Trent End
Capacity of Stand: -

ADMISSION INFO (1993/94 PRICES)
Adult Seating: £12.00 - £14.00
Child Seating: £8.00 (Family Section Only)
Programme Price: £1.20
FAX Number: (0602) 526003

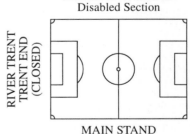

Travelling Supporters Information:
Routes: From North: Exit M1 junction 26 following Nottingham signs (A610) then Melton Mowbray and Trent Bridge (A606) signs. Cross River Trent, left into Radcliffe Road then left into Colwick Road; From South: Exit M1 junction 24 following signs Nottingham (South) to Trent Bridge. Turn right into Radcliffe Road then left into Colwick Road; From East: Take A52 to West Bridgford, turn right into Colwick Road; From West: Take A52 into Nottingham following signs Melton Mowbray and Trent Bridge; cross River Trent (then as North).

NOTTS COUNTY FC

Founded: 1862 (Oldest in League)	**Record Attendance**: 47,310 (12/3/55)
Turned Professional: 1885	**Colours**: Shirts - Black and White Stripes
Limited Company: 1888	Amber Sleeve & Trim
Admitted to League: 1888 (Founder)	Shorts - Black
Former Name(s): None	**Telephone No.**: (0602) 861155
Nickname: 'Magpies'	**Ticket Information**: (0602) 861155/850632
Ground: Meadow Lane, Nottingham	**Pitch Size**: 117 × 76yds
NG2 3HJ	**Ground Capacity**: 20,307
	Seating Capacity: 20,307

GENERAL INFORMATION
Supporters Club Administrator:
P. Dennis
Address: c/o Club
Telephone Number: (0602) 866802
Car Parking: British Waterways, Meadow Lane
Coach Parking: Incinerator Road (Cattle Market Corner)
Nearest Railway Station: Nottingham Midland (0.5 mile)
Nearest Bus Station: Broadmarsh Centre
Club Shop:
Opening Times: Weekdays & Matchdays 9.00-5.30pm. Other Saturdays 9.00-12.00
Telephone No.: (0602) 861155
Postal Sales: Yes
Nearest Police Station: Station Street, Nottingham
Police Force: Nottinghamshire
Police Telephone No.: (0602) 481888

GROUND INFORMATION
Away Supporters' Entrances: Cattle Market Corner, Iremonger Road
Away Supporters' Sections: The Kop Stand
Family Facilities: **Location of Stand**:
Family Stand - Meadow Lane End
Capacity of Stand: 2,139

ADMISSION INFO (1994/95 PRICES)
Adult Seating: £10.00 - £14.00
Child Seating: £5.00
Programme Price: £1.20
FAX Number: (0602) 866442

JIMMY SIRRELL STAND
Disabled

(CATTLE MARKET ROAD)
THE KOP STAND (Away)

(SPORTS CENTRE)
MEADOW LANE
FAMILY STAND

DEREK PAVIS STAND

Travelling Supporters Information:
Routes: From North: Exit M1 junction 26 following Nottingham signs (A610) then Melton Mowbray and Trent Bridge (A606) signs. Before River Trent turn left into Meadow Lane; From South: Exit M1 junction 24 following signs Nottingham (South) to Trent Bridge, cross River and follow one-way system to the right, then turn left and right at traffic lights then second right into Meadow Lane; From East: Take A52 to West Bridgford/Trent Bridge, cross River and follow one-way system to the right then turn left and right at traffic lights, then second right into Meadow Lane; From West: Take A52 into Nottingham following signs Melton Mowbray and Trent Bridge, before River Trent turn left into Meadow Lane.

OLDHAM ATHLETIC FC

Founded: 1895
Turned Professional: 1899
Limited Company: 1906
Admitted to League: 1907
Former Name(s): Pine Villa FC (1895-99)
Nickname: 'Latics'
Ground: Boundary Park, Oldham   OL1 2PA

Record Attendance: 47,671 (25/1/30)
Colours: Shirts - Blue
               Shorts - Blue
Telephone No.: (061) 624-4972 (24 hours)
Ticket Information: (061) 624-4972
Pitch Size: 110 × 74yds
Ground Capacity: 13,544
Seating Capacity: 13,544

GENERAL INFORMATION
Supporters Club Administrator: John Stanley
Address: c/o Club
Telephone Number: (061) 624-4972
Car Parking: Lookers Stand Car Park (1,000 cars)
Coach Parking: At Ground
Nearest Railway Station: Oldham Werneth (1.5 miles)
Nearest Bus Station: Oldham Mumps (2 miles)
Club Shop:
Opening Times: Mondays-Saturdays 9.00-5.00
Telephone No.: (061) 652-0966
Postal Sales: Yes
Nearest Police Station: Chadderton
Police Force: Greater Manchester
Police Telephone No.: (061) 624-0444

GROUND INFORMATION
Away Supporters' Entrances: Rochdale Road Turnstiles
Away Supporters' Sections: Rochdale Road Stand (seating)
Family Facilities: Location of Stand: Lookers Stand
Capacity of Stand: 1,433

ADMISSION INFO (1994/95 PRICES)
Adult Seating: £7.50 - £13.00   (Away Fans £12.00)
Child Seating: £6.50 - £8.00   (Away Fans £8.00)
Programme Price: £1.30
FAX Number: (061) 627-5915

LOOKERS STAND

SETON STAND

ROCHDALE ROAD STAND (Away)

GEORGE HILL STAND

Travelling Supporters Information:
Routes: From All Parts: Exit M62 junction 20 and take A627M to junction with A664. Take 1st exit at roundabout on to Broadway, then 1st right into Hilbre Avenue which leads to car park.

OXFORD UNITED FC

Founded: 1893
Turned Professional: 1949
Limited Company: 1949
Admitted to League: 1962
Former Name(s): Headington United FC (1893-1960)
Nickname: 'U's'
Ground: Manor Ground, London Road, Headington, Oxford OX3 7RS

Record Attendance: 22,730 (29/2/64)
Colours: Shirts - Yellow with Navy Trim
Shorts - Navy with Yellow Trim
Telephone No.: (0865) 61503
Ticket Information: (0865) 61503
Pitch Size: 110 × 75yds
Ground Capacity: 11,071
Seating Capacity: 2,777

GENERAL INFORMATION

Supporters Club Administrator: Gary Whiting
Address: c/o Club
Telephone Number: (0865) 63063
Car Parking: Street Parking
Coach Parking: Off Headley Way in Franklin Road
Nearest Railway Station: Oxford (3 miles)
Nearest Bus Station: Queen's Lane (2 miles)
Club Shop: 67 London Road, Headington
Opening Times: Monday-Saturday 9.30-5.30 (closes 3.00pm Matchdays)
Telephone No.: (0865) 61503
Postal Sales: Members only
Nearest Police Station: Cowley (2 miles)
Police Force: Thames Valley
Police Telephone No.: (0865) 749909

GROUND INFORMATION

Away Supporters' Entrances: Cuckoo Lane Turnstiles 5-11
Away Supporters' Sections: Cuckoo Lane Stand
Family Facilities: **Location of Stand**:
Beech Road Side (Members only)
Capacity of Stand: 162 uncovered seating, 306 covered seating

ADMISSION INFO (1994/95 PRICES)

Adult Standing: £7 - £8 (£6 - £7 members)
Adult Seating: £9.00 - £11.00
Child Standing: £4.50 - £5 (£3.00 - £3.50 members)
Child Seating: £4.50 - £7.50
Programme Price: £1.30
FAX Number: (0865) 741820

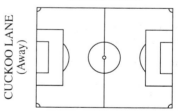

OSLER ROAD
CUCKOO LANE (Away)
LONDON ROAD
Disabled Section   BEECH ROAD

Travelling Supporters Information:
Routes: From North: Exit M40 at Junction 9. Follow signs for A34 to Oxford. Take slip road A44 marked Witney, Woodstock. At roundabout take first exit (Pear Tree). Follow to next roundabout A44 junction with A40 Woodstock Road, take second exit marked A40 London. Down to next roundabout (Banbury Road), take second exit on to Northern by-pass. Cars should take next left turn at slip road marked New Marston 0.5 mile and JR Hospital 1 mile. (Coaches should follow diversions to avoid weak bridge, next roundabout A40 (Green Road), take fifth exit, follow signs for A40 junction with B4105 Marston.) Down to mini roundabout turn left. Straight up Headley Way, coaches should take second junction right marked Franklin Road which leads into Coach park. Cars - side street parking only. Take care for matchday parking restrictions. From South: A34 by-pass to junction A44 Pear Tree. Then as North. From East: Cars & Coaches should follow diversion directions as from Green Road Roundabout. From West: Take A34 following signs to M40. Take exit A44 marked Woodstock, take third exit Pear Tree, then as North.
Bus Services: Service 1 Railway Station to Queen's Lane, Service 2 to Ground.

PETERBOROUGH UNITED FC

Founded: 1923
Turned Professional: 1934
Limited Company: 1934
Admitted to League: 1960
Former Name(s): Peterborough & Fletton United FC (1923-34)
Nickname: 'Posh'
Ground: London Road, Peterborough, Cambs   PE2 8AL

Record Attendance: 30,096 (20/2/65)
Colours: Shirts - Blue
Shorts - White
Telephone No.: (0733) 63947
Ticket Information: (0733) 63947
Pitch Size: 112 × 72yds
Ground Capacity: 18,978 (Being reviewed)
Seating Capacity: 4,715

GENERAL INFORMATION
Supporters Club Administrator: Ray Duke
Address: c/o Club
Telephone Number: -
Car Parking: Ample Parking at Ground
Coach Parking: Rear of Ground
Nearest Railway Station: Peterborough (1 mile)
Nearest Bus Station: Peterborough (0.25 mile)
Club Shop:
Opening Times: Monday-Friday 9.00-5.00
Telephone No.: (0733) 69760
Postal Sales: Yes
Nearest Police Station: Bridge Street, Peterborough (5 minutes walk)
Police Force: Cambridgeshire
Police Telephone No.: (0733) 63232

GROUND INFORMATION
Away Supporters' Entrances: Turnstile A, Moys End
Away Supporters' Sections: Moys End (Covered Standing) - Block A seating
Family Facilities: Location of Stand:

Capacity of Stand: -
ADMISSION INFO (1994/95 PRICES)
Adult Standing: £7.50
Adult Seating: £12.00 (Wings End £10.00)
Child Standing: £3.50 (Home fans only)
Child Seating: £6.00   (Wings End £5.00)
Programme Price: £1.00
FAX Number: (0733) 557210

GLEBE ROAD

MOYS END (Away)

LONDON ROAD

EAST STAND   Disabled
SEATED ENCLOSURE

Travelling Supporters Information:
Routes: From North & West: Take A1 then A47 into Town Centre, follow Whittlesey signs across river into London Road; From East: Take A47 into Town Centre (then as North); From South: Take A1 then A15 into London Road.

PLYMOUTH ARGYLE FC

Founded: 1886
Turned Professional: 1903
Limited Company: 1903
Admitted to League: 1920
Former Name(s): Argyle FC (1886-1903)
Nickname: 'Pilgrims'   'Argyle'
Ground: Home Park, Plymouth   PL2 3DQ

Record Attendance: 43,596 (10/10/36)
Colours: Shirts - Green & Black Stripes
Shorts - Black
Telephone No.: (0752) 562561
Ticket Information: (0752) 562561
Pitch Size: 112 × 72yds
Ground Capacity: 19,900
Seating Capacity: 6,700

GENERAL INFORMATION
Supporters Club Administrator:
S. Rendell
Address: c/o Club
Telephone Number: (0752) 562561
Car Parking: Car Park (1,000 Cars) Adjacent
Coach Parking: Central Car Park
Nearest Railway Station: Plymouth North Road
Nearest Bus Station: Bretonside, Plymouth
Club Shop:
Opening Times: Monday-Saturday 9.00-5.00
Telephone No.: (0752) 558292
Postal Sales: Yes
Nearest Police Station: Devonport (1 mile)
Police Force: Devon & Cornwall
Police Telephone No.: (0752) 701188

GROUND INFORMATION
Away Supporters' Entrances: Barn Park End Turnstiles (standing)
Away Supporters' Sections: Barn Park End (Open)
Family Facilities: Location of Stand:
Devonport End of Grandstand
Capacity of Stand: 600

ADMISSION INFO (1994/95 PRICES)
Adult Standing: £5.50 or £6.00
Adult Seating: £8.00 - £10.00
Child Standing: £3.50
Child Seating: £6.00
Programme Price: £1.30
FAX Number: (0752) 606167
Note: There are special rates for adults & children in the Family Enclosure (Prices shown are for category 'A' games - category 'B' & 'C' games will be at a higher price).

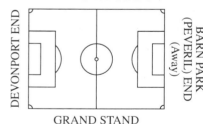

TAVISTOCK ROAD
LYNDHURST STAND

DEVONPORT END

BARN PARK
(PEVERIL) END
(Away)

GRAND STAND

Travelling Supporters Information:
Routes: From All Parts: Take A38 to Tavistock Road (A386), then branch left following signs Plymouth (A386), continue for 1.25 miles - car park on left (signposted Home Park).

PORTSMOUTH FC

Founded: 1898
Turned Professional: 1898
Limited Company: 1898
Admitted to League: 1920
Former Name(s): None
Nickname: 'Pompey'
Ground: Fratton Park, 57 Frogmore Road, Portsmouth, Hants   PO4 8RA

Record Attendance: 51,385 (26/2/49)
Colours: Shirts - Blue
Shorts - White
Telephone No.: (0705) 731204
Ticket Information: (0705) 750825
Pitch Size: 114 × 72yds
Ground Capacity: 26,452
Seating Capacity: 7,000

GENERAL INFORMATION
Supporters Club Administrator: -
Address: c/o Club
Telephone Number: -
Car Parking: Street Parking
Coach Parking: By Police Direction
Nearest Railway Station: Fratton (Adjacent)
Nearest Bus Station: Hilsea
Club Shop:
Opening Times: Monday-Friday 9.00-5.00
Saturdays 10.00-2.00
Telephone No.: (0705) 738358
Postal Sales: Yes
Nearest Police Station: Southsea
Police Force: Hampshire
Police Telephone No.: (0705) 321111

GROUND INFORMATION
Away Supporters' Entrances: Aspley Road - Milton Road side
Away Supporters' Sections: Aspley Road End (Open)
Family Facilities: **Location of Stand**:
2 - South Enclosure, Carisbrooke Road & 'G' Section, Milton Road
Capacity of Stand: 3,300 (S);   3,200 (N)

ADMISSION INFO (1994/95 PRICES)
Adult Standing: £8.00
Adult Seating: £11.00 - £15.00
Child Standing: £5.00
Child Seating: £5.00 - £7.00
Programme Price: £1.20
FAX Number: (0705) 734129

Travelling Supporters Information:
Routes: From North & West: Take M27 and M275 to end then take 2nd exit at roundabout and in 0.25 mile turn right at 'T' junction into London Road (A2047), in 1.25 mile cross railway bridge and turn left into Goldsmith Avenue. After 0.5 mile turn left into Frogmore Road; From East: Take A27 following Southsea signs (A2030). Turn left at roundabout (3 miles) into A288, then right into Priory Crescent and next right into Carisbrooke Road.

PORT VALE FC

Founded: 1876	**Record Attendance**: 50,000 (20/2/60)
Turned Professional: 1885	**Colours**: Shirts - White
Limited Company: 1911	Shorts - Black
Admitted to League: 1892	**Telephone No.**: (0782) 814134
Former Name(s): Burslem Port Vale FC	**Ticket Information**: (0782) 814134
(1876-1913)	**Pitch Size**: 114 × 77yds
Nickname: 'Valiants'	**Ground Capacity**: 22,359
Ground: Vale Park, Burslem, Stoke-on-Trent,	**Seating Capacity**: 12,442
ST6 1AW	

GENERAL INFORMATION
Supporters Club Administrator:
John Greatbatch
Address: Port Vale Supporters' Group,
90 Park Lane, Knypersley, Stoke ST8 7BQ
Telephone Number: (0782) 514721
Car Parking: Car Parks at Ground
Coach Parking: Hamil Road Car Park
Nearest Railway Station: Stoke
Nearest Bus Station: Burslem
Adjacent
Club Shop:
Opening Times: Monday-Saturday 9.00-5.30
Telephone No.: (0782) 835524
Postal Sales: Yes
Nearest Police Station: Burslem
Police Force: Staffordshire
Police Telephone No.: (0782) 577114

GROUND INFORMATION
Away Supporters' Entrances: Hamil Road turnstiles
Away Supporters' Sections: Hamil Road End
Family Facilities: Location of Stand:
Railway Stand/Bycars Corner
Capacity of Stand: 500 seats ; 470 terracing

ADMISSION INFO (1994/95 PRICES)
Adult Standing: £6.00 - £7.50
Adult Seating: £8.50 - £10.00
Child Standing: £3.50 or £5.00
Child Seating: £4.50 - £7.50
Programme Price: £1.20
FAX Number: (0782) 834981

RAILWAY STAND
(Family Stand)

(CAR PARK) HAMIL ROAD (Away)

BYCARS STAND

(Disabled) LORNE STREET
← BUS

Travelling Supporters Information:
Routes: From North: Exit M6 junction 16 and follow Stoke signs (A500). Branch left off the A500 at the exit signposted Tunstall and take 1st exit at roundabout onto A50. Turn right 0.25 mile into Newcastle Street and at end cross into Moorland Road. Then turn left into Hamil Road; From South & West: Exit M6 junction 15 and take A5006 and A500, after 6.25 miles branch left (then as North); From East: Take A50 or A52 into Stoke following Burslem signs into Waterloo Road, turn right at Burslem crossroads into Moorland Road (then as North).

PRESTON NORTH END FC

Founded: 1881
Turned Professional: 1885
Limited Company: 1893
Admitted to League: 1888
Nickname: 'Lilywhites'   'North End'
Ground: Deepdale, Preston   PR1 6RU
Record Attendance: 42,684 (23/4/38)

Colours: Shirts - White with Navy Trim
Shorts - Blue
Telephone No.: (0772) 795919
Ticket Information: (0772) 795919
Pitch Size: 110 × 72yds
Ground Capacity: 16,249
Seating Capacity: 3,000

GENERAL INFORMATION
Supporters Club Administrator:
Maureen Robinson
Address: 40 Southgate, Fulwood, Preston
Telephone Number: (0772) 774005
Car Parking: West Stand Car Park (600 cars)
Coach Parking: West Stand Car Park
Nearest Railway Station: Preston (2 miles)
Nearest Bus Station: Preston (1 mile)
Club Shop:
Opening Times: Weekdays 9.00-5.00
Matchdays 12.30-5.00
Telephone No.: (0772) 795465
Postal Sales: Yes
Nearest Police Station: Lawson Street,
Preston (1 mile)
Police Force: Lancashire
Police Telephone No.: (0772) 203203

GROUND INFORMATION
Away Supporters' Entrances: West Stand Turnstiles
Away Supporters' Sections: West Stand Paddock
Family Facilities: Location of Stand:
West Stand
Capacity of Stand: 300

ADMISSION INFO (1994/95 PRICES)
Adult Standing: £5.00 or £5.50 (Away fans £6.50)
Adult Seating: £7.00 or £8.00   (Away fans £8.00)
Child Standing: £2.50 or £3.50 (Away fans £4.50)
Child Seating: £4.00 or £5.00 (Away fans £6.00)
Programme Price: £1.20
FAX Number: (0772) 653266
Note: If the team is Seventh or higher in the League,
adult home fans are charged £1.00 extra.

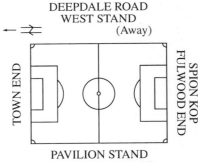

DEEPDALE ROAD
WEST STAND
(Away)

TOWN END

SPION KOP
FULWOOD END

PAVILION STAND
LOWTHORPE ROAD

Travelling Supporters Information:
Routes: From North: M6 then M55 to junction 1. Follow signs to Preston A6. After 2 miles turn left at the crossroads into Blackpool Road (A5085). Turn right 0.75 mile into Deepdale; From South & East: Exit M6 junction 31 and follow Preston signs (A59). Take 2nd exit at roundabout (1 mile) into Blackpool Road. Turn left (1.25 mile) into Deepdale; From West: Exit M55 junction 1 (then as North).

QUEEN'S PARK RANGERS FC

Founded: 1882
Turned Professional: 1898
Limited Company: 1899
Admitted to League: 1920
Former Name(s): Formed by amalgamation of St. Jude's & Christchurch Rangers FC
Nickname: 'Rangers' 'R's'
Ground: Rangers Stadium, South Africa Road London W12 7PA

Record Attendance: 35,353 (27/4/74)
Colours: Shirts - Blue and White Hoops
   Shorts - White
Telephone No.: (081) 743-0262
Ticket Information: (081) 743-0262
Pitch Size: 110 × 75yds
Ground Capacity: 19,200
Seating Capacity: 19,200

GENERAL INFORMATION
Supporters Club Administrator:
Patricia Dix
Address: c/o Club
Telephone Number: (081) 749-6771
Car Parking: Street Parking
Coach Parking: By Police Direction
Nearest Railway Station: Shepherd's Bush
Nearest Tube Station: White City (Central)
Club Shop:
Opening Times: Monday-Friday 9.00-5.00
Saturday 9.00am-12.30pm
Telephone No.: (081) 749-6862
Postal Sales: Yes
Nearest Police Station: Uxbridge Road, Shepherd's Bush (0.5 mile)
Police Force: Metropolitan
Police Telephone No.: (081) 741-6212

GROUND INFORMATION
Away Supporters' Entrances: South Africa Road, Turnstiles 29-34 & Ellerslie Road, Nºs 35-37
Away Supporters' Sections: School End Stand (Partially covered)
Family Facilities: **Location of Stand**: Loftus Road Stand
Capacity of Stand: 3,152 seating

ADMISSION INFO (1994/95 PRICES)
Adult Seating: £11.00 - £25.00
Child Seating: £11.00 - £25.00
Programme Price: £1.50
FAX Number: (081) 749-0994
Note : Prices vary depending on opponents. No Child concessions for Category 'A' games

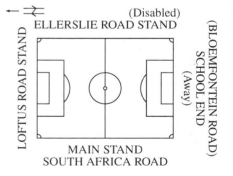

(Disabled)
ELLERSLIE ROAD STAND
ELLERSLIE ROAD STAND (Disabled)
LOFTUS ROAD STAND
(BLOEMFONTEIN ROAD) SCHOOL END (Away)
MAIN STAND
SOUTH AFRICA ROAD

Travelling Supporters Information:
Routes: From North: Take M1 & A406 North Circular for Neasden, turn left 0.75 mile (A404) following signs Harlesden, then Hammersmith, past White City Stadium and right into White City Road, then left into South Africa Road; From South: Take A206, A3 across Putney Bridge following signs to Hammersmith, then Oxford A219 to Shepherd's Bush to join A4020 following signs to Acton, in 0.25 mile turn right into Loftus Road; From East: Take A12, A406 then A503 to join Ring Road follow Oxford signs to join A40(M), branch left (2 miles) to M41, 3rd exit at roundabout to A4020 (then as South); From West: Take M4 to Chiswick then A315 and A402 to Shepherd's Bush, join A4020 (then as South).

READING FC

Founded: 1871	**Record Attendance**: 33,042 (19/2/27)
Turned Professional: 1895	**Colours**: Shirts - Navy & White
Limited Company: 1897	Shorts - White
Admitted to League: 1920	**Telephone No.**: (0734) 507878
Former Name(s): Amalgamated with Hornets	**Ticket Information**: (0734) 507878
FC (1877) and Earley FC (1889)	**Pitch Size**: 112 × 77yds
Nickname: 'Royals'	**Ground Capacity**: 12,134
Ground: Elm Park, Norfolk Road, Reading,	**Seating Capacity**: 2,100
RG3 2EF	

GENERAL INFORMATION
Supporters Club Administrator: -
Address: -
Telephone Number: -
Car Parking: Street Parking/Prospect School
Coach Parking: The Meadway
Nearest Railway Station: Reading West (0.5 mile)
Nearest Bus Station: Reading
Club Shop: Via Ticket Office
Opening Times: Monday-Friday & Matchdays 9.00-5.00pm
Telephone No.: (0734) 507878
Postal Sales: Yes
Nearest Police Station: Castle Street, Reading (2 miles)
Police Force: Thames Valley
Police Telephone No.: (0734) 536000

GROUND INFORMATION
Away Supporters' Entrances: Norfolk Road Turnstiles
Away Supporters' Sections: Reading End/Norfolk Road (Open Terrace) + 'A' Stand Seating
Family Facilities: **Location of Stand**: Norfolk Road side 'E' Stand
Capacity of Stand: 299

ADMISSION INFO (1994/95 PRICES)
Adult Standing: £7.50
Adult Seating: £9.00 - £11.00
Child Standing: £5.00 (Home fans only)
Child Seating: £5.00 (Family Stand only)
Programme Price: £1.20
FAX Number: (0734) 566628

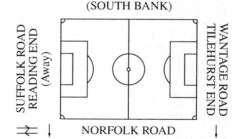

Travelling Supporters Information:
Routes: From North: Take A423, A4074 and A4155 from Oxford across railway bridge into Reading. Follow signs for Newbury (A4) into Castle Hill, then right into Tilehurst Road. Turn right after 0.75 mile into Cranbury Road then left and 2nd left into Norfolk Road; From South: Take A33 into Reading and follow Newbury signs into Bath Road. Cross railway bridge and take 3rd right into Liebenrood Road. At the end turn right into Tilehurst Road then 1st left into Cranbury Road and 2nd left into Norfolk Road; From East: Exit M4 junction 10 and use A329 and A4 into Reading. Cross railway bridge (then as South); From West: Exit M4 junction 12 and take A4. After 3.25 miles turn left into Liebenrood Road (then as South).

ROCHDALE FC

Founded: 1907	**Record Attendance**: 24,231 (10/12/49)
Turned Professional: 1907	**Colours**: Shirts - Blue & White
Limited Company: 1910	Shorts - Blue & White
Admitted to League: 1921	**Telephone No.**: (0706) 44648
Former Name(s): Rochdale Town FC	**Ticket Information**: (0706) 44648
Nickname: 'The Dale'	**Pitch Size**: 114 × 76yds
Ground: Willbutts Lane, Spotland, Rochdale	**Ground Capacity**: 7,564
OL11 5DS	**Seating Capacity**: 1,852

GENERAL INFORMATION

Supporters Club Administrator:
F. Duffy
Address: c/o Club
Telephone Number: (0706) 852498
Car Parking: Car Park at Ground
Coach Parking: By Police Direction
Nearest Railway Station: Rochdale (2 miles)
Nearest Bus Station: Town Centre (1 mile)
Club Shop:
Opening Times: Weekdays 9.15-5.30 and Matchdays 9.15-6.00
Telephone No.: (0706) 47521
Postal Sales: Yes
Nearest Police Station: Rochdale (1.5 miles)
Police Force: Greater Manchester
Police Telephone No.: (0706) 47401

GROUND INFORMATION

Away Supporters' Entrances: Pearl Street Turnstiles
Away Supporters' Sections: Pearl St. End (Open & Covered)
Family Facilities: **Location of Stand**:
Main Stand - Blocks F & G
Capacity of Stand: 636

ADMISSION INFO (1994/95 PRICES)

Adult Standing: £6.00
Adult Seating: £8.00
Child Standing: £3.00
Child Seating: £4.50
Programme Price: £1.20
FAX Number: (0706) 48466

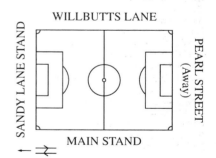

Travelling Supporters Information:

Routes: From North, South, East & West: Exit M62 junction 20 following Rochdale signs, take 2nd exit at 2nd roundabout (1.5 miles) into Roch Valley Way signed Blackburn. At next traffic lights go straight ahead and ground is on right in 0.5 miles.

ROTHERHAM UNITED FC

Founded: 1884
Turned Professional: 1905
Limited Company: 1920
Admitted to League: 1893
Former Name(s): Thornhill United FC (1884-1905); Rotherham County FC (1905-1925)
Nickname: 'The Merry Millers'
Ground: Millmoor Ground, Rotherham S60 1HR

Record Attendance: 25,000 (13/12/52)
Colours: Shirts - Red
Shorts - White
Telephone No.: (0709) 562434
Ticket Information: (0709) 562434
Pitch Size: 115 × 76yds
Ground Capacity: 11,533
Seating Capacity: 3,407

GENERAL INFORMATION
Supporters Club Administrator:
Mrs R. Cowley
Address: 50 Lister Street, Rotherham
Telephone Number: (0709) 375831
Car Parking: Kimberworth Road and Main Street Car Parks
Coach Parking: By Police Direction
Nearest Railway Station: Rotherham Central (0.5 mile)
Nearest Bus Station: Town Centre (0.5 mile)
Club Shop:
Opening Times: Monday-Saturday 9.00-5.00
Telephone No.: (0709) 562760
Postal Sales: Yes
Nearest Police Station: Rotherham (0.5 mile)
Police Force: South Yorkshire
Police Telephone No.: (0709) 371121

GROUND INFORMATION
Away Supporters' Entrances: Millmoor Lane Turnstiles
Away Supporters' Sections: Millmoor Lane/Railway End
Family Facilities: Location of Stand: Millmoor Lane Side
Capacity of Stand: 748

ADMISSION INFO (1994/95 PRICES)
Adult Standing: £6.00 (Away Supporters £7.00)
Adult Seating: £7.00 - £8.50
Child Standing: £4.00
Child Seating: £4.50 - £5.50
Programme Price: £1.20
FAX Number: (0709) 563336

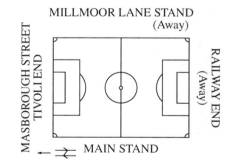

MILLMOOR LANE STAND
(Away)

MASBOROUGH STREET
TIVOLI END

RAILWAY END
(Away)

MAIN STAND

Travelling Supporters Information:
Routes: From North: Exit M1 junction 34 following Rotherham (A6109) signs to traffic lights and turn right into Millmoor Lane. Ground is 0.24 mile on right over railway bridge; From South & West: Exit M1 junction 33, turn right following 'Rotherham' signs. Turn left at roundabout and right at next roundabout. Follow dual carriageway to next roundabout and go straight on. Turn left at next roundabout and ground is 0.25 mile on left; From East: Take A630 into Rotherham following Sheffield signs. At 2nd roundabout turn right into Masborough Street then 1st left into Millmoor Lane.

SCARBOROUGH FC

Founded: 1879
Limited Company: 1933
Admitted to League: 1987
Former Name(s): None
Nickname: 'Boro'
Ground: McCain Stadium, Seamer Road, Scarborough, N.Yorks YO12 4HF

Record Attendance: 11,124 (1938)
Colours: Shirts - Red
Shorts - White
Telephone No.: (0723) 375094
Ticket Information: (0723) 375094
Pitch Size: 112 × 74yds
Ground Capacity: 6,899
Seating Capacity: 808

GENERAL INFORMATION
Social Club Administrator: Mrs.S.Nettleton
Address: c/o Club
Telephone Number: (0723) 375094
Car Parking: Street Parking
Coach Parking: Scarborough Coach Park
Nearest Railway Station: Scarborough Central (2 miles)
Nearest Bus Station: Westwood Scarborough (2 miles)
Club Shop:
Opening Times: Weekdays 9.30-5.00pm & Matchdays
Telephone No.: (0723) 375094
Postal Sales: Yes
Nearest Police Station: Scarborough (2 mls)
Police Force: North Yorkshire
Police Telephone No.: (0723) 500300

GROUND INFORMATION
Away Supporters' Entrances: Edgehill Road Turnstiles
Away Supporters' Sections: Visitors Enclosure, Edgehill Road End
Family Facilities: **Location of Stand**:

Capacity of Stand: -

ADMISSION INFO (1994/95 PRICES)
Adult Standing: £5.00
Adult Seating: £7.50
Child Standing: £2.50
Child Seating: £5.00
Programme Price: £1.00
FAX Number: (0723) 378733

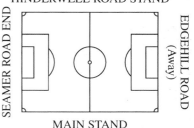

Travelling Supporters Information:
Routes: The Ground is situated on the main York to Scarborough Road (A64) 0.5 mile on left past B & Q DIY Store.

SCUNTHORPE UNITED FC

Founded: 1899	**Record Attendance**: 8,775 (1/5/89)
Turned Professional: 1912	**Colours**: Shirts - White with Claret/Blue Trim
Limited Company: 1912	Shorts - Sky Blue + Claret/Blue Trim
Admitted to League: 1950	**Telephone No.**: (0724) 848077
Former Name(s): Scunthorpe & Lindsey	**Ticket Information**: (0724) 848077
United (1899-1912)	**Pitch Size**: 111 × 73yds
Nickname: 'Irons'	**Ground Capacity**: 9,200
Ground: Glanford Park, Doncaster Road,	**Seating Capacity**: 6,400
Scunthorpe, South Humberside DN15 8TD	

GENERAL INFORMATION
Supporters Club Administrator:
A. Webster
Address: 72 Byfield Road, Scunthorpe
Telephone Number: (0724) 863009
Car Parking: For 600 cars at Ground
Coach Parking: At Ground
Nearest Railway Station: Scunthorpe
(1.5 miles)
Nearest Bus Station: Scunthorpe (1.5 miles)
Club Shop:
Opening Times: Weekdays 9.00-5.00
Matchdays 10.30-5.00
Telephone No.: (0724) 848077
Postal Sales: Yes
Nearest Police Station: Laneham Street,
Scunthorpe (1.5 miles)
Police Force: Humberside
Police Telephone No.: (0724) 282888

GROUND INFORMATION
Away Supporters' Entrances: Turnstiles 6-7
Away Supporters' Sections: South Stand
Family Facilities: Location of Stand:
Clugston Stand
Capacity of Stand: 2,277

ADMISSION INFO (1994/95 PRICES)
Adult Standing: £6.00
Adult Seating: £7.50 - £8.50
Child Standing: £3.00
Child Seating: £3.70 or £5.50
Programme Price: £1.30
FAX Number: (0724) 857986

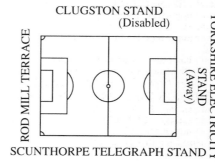

CLUGSTON STAND
(Disabled)

ROD MILL TERRACE

YORKSHIRE ELECTRICITY STAND (Away)

SCUNTHORPE TELEGRAPH STAND

Travelling Supporters Information:
Routes: From All Parts: Exit M180 junction 3 onto M181. Follow M181 to roundabout with A18 and take A18 towards Scunthorpe - Ground on right next to roundabout (200 yards).

SHEFFIELD UNITED FC

Founded: 1889
Turned Professional: 1889
Limited Company: 1899
Admitted to League: 1892
Former Name(s): None
Nickname: 'Blades'
Ground: Bramall Lane, Sheffield   S2 4SU

Record Attendance: 68,287 (15/2/36)
Colours: Shirts - Red & White Stripes with Black Pinstripe
Shorts - Black
Telephone No.: (0742) 738955
Ticket Information: (0742) 766771
Pitch Size: 113 × 72yds
Ground Capacity: 23,314
Seating Capacity: 23,314

GENERAL INFORMATION
Supporters Club Administrator:
Beryl Whitney
Address: 42 Base Green Avenue, Sheffield S12 3FA
Telephone Number: (0742) 390202
Car Parking: Street Parking
Coach Parking: By Police Direction
Nearest Railway Station: Sheffield Midland (1 mile)
Nearest Bus Station: Pond Street, Sheffield
Club Shop:
Opening Times: Monday-Friday 9.30-5.00
Matchdays 9.30-5.30
Telephone No.: (0742) 750596
Postal Sales: Yes
Nearest Police Station: Police Room at Ground
Police Force: South Yorkshire
Police Telephone No.: (0742) 768522

GROUND INFORMATION
Away Supporters' Entrances: Bramall Lane Turnstiles
Away Supporters' Sections: Bramall Lane Upper Stand
Family Facilities: Location of Stand:
New South Stand - West Wing - Membership Area
Capacity of Stand: 2,000 (Family Section)

ADMISSION INFO (1994/95 PRICES)
Adult Seating: £9.00 - £14.00
Child Seating: £6.00 - £7.00
Programme Price: £1.20
FAX Number: (0742) 723030

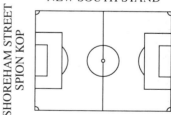

Travelling Supporters Information:
Routes: From North: Exit M1 junction 34 following signs to Sheffield (A6109), turn left 3.5 miles and take 4th exit at roundabout into Sheaf Street. Take 5th exit at 2nd roundabout into St. Mary's Road (for Bakewell), turn left 0.5 mile into Bramall Lane; From South & East: Exit M1 junctions 31 or 33 and take A57 to roundabout, take 3rd exit into Sheaf Street (then as North); From West: Take A57 into Sheffield and take 4th exit at roundabout into Upper Hanover Street and at 2nd roundabout take 3rd exit into Bramall Lane.

SHEFFIELD WEDNESDAY FC

Founded: 1867
Turned Professional: 1887
Limited Company: 1899
Admitted to League: 1892
Former Name(s): The Wednesday FC
Nickname: 'Owls'
Ground: Hillsborough, Sheffield   S6 1SW

Record Attendance: 72,841 (17/2/34)
Colours: Shirts - Blue & White Stripes
Shorts - Black
Telephone No.: (0742) 343122
Ticket Information: (0742) 337233
Pitch Size: 115 × 75yds
Ground Capacity: 36,020
Seating Capacity: 36,020

GENERAL INFORMATION
Supporters Club Administrator:
Mrs Nettleship
Address: c/o Club
Telephone Number: (0742) 333419
Car Parking: Street Parking
Coach Parking: Owlerton Stadium
Nearest Railway Station: Sheffield (4 miles)
Nearest Bus Station: Sheffield (4 miles)
Club Shop:
Opening Times: Monday-Saturday
10.00-4.30
Telephone No.: (0742) 343342
Postal Sales: Yes
Nearest Police Station: Hammerton Road,
Sheffield (1 mile)
Police Force: South Yorkshire
Police Telephone No.: (0742) 343131

GROUND INFORMATION
Away Supporters' Entrances: West Stand Turnstiles
Away Supporters' Sections: West Stand -Upper Tier
Family Facilities: **Location of Stand**:
Penistone Road Wing
Capacity of Stand: Approximately 1,000

ADMISSION INFO (1994/95 PRICES)
Adult Seating: £8.00 - £16.00
Child Seating: £5.00 - £11.50
Programme Price: £1.30
FAX Number: (0742) 337145
(Prices depend on category of game)

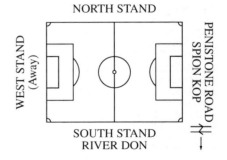

Travelling Supporters Information:
Routes: From North: Exit M1 junction 34 following signs for Sheffield (A6109), take 3rd exit (1.5 miles) at roundabout and in 3.25 miles turn left into Herries Road for Ground; From South & East: Exit M1 junctions 31 or 33 and take A57 to roundabout, take exit into Prince of Wales Road after 5.75 miles turn left into Herries Road South; From West: Take A57 until A6101 and turn left. After 3.75 miles turn left at 'T' junction into Penistone Road for Ground.

SHREWSBURY TOWN FC

Founded: 1886	**Record Attendance**: 18,917 (26/4/61)
Turned Professional: 1905	**Colours**: Shirts - Blue, Yellow & White
Limited Company: 1936	Shorts - Blue, Yellow & White
Admitted to League: 1950	**Telephone No.**: (0743) 360111
Former Name(s): None	**Ticket Information**: (0743) 360111
Nickname: 'Town'	**Pitch Size**: 116 × 75yds
Ground: Gay Meadow, Shrewsbury	**Ground Capacity**: 8,000
SY2 6AB	**Seating Capacity**: 3,000

GENERAL INFORMATION
Supporters Club Administrator: Fred Brown
Address: c/o Club
Telephone Number: (0743) 360111
Car Parking: Car Park Adjacent
Coach Parking: Gay Meadow
Nearest Railway Station: Shrewsbury (1 mile)
Nearest Bus Station: Baker Street, Shrewsbury
Club Shop:
Opening Times: Matchdays & Office Hours
Telephone No.: (0743) 356316
Postal Sales: Yes
Nearest Police Station: Clive Road, Shrewsbury
Police Force: West Mercia
Police Telephone No.: (0743) 232888

GROUND INFORMATION
Away Supporters' Entrances: Station End Turnstiles
Away Supporters' Sections: Station Stand (Covered)
Family Facilities: Location of Stand: Wakeman Stand
Capacity of Stand: 500

ADMISSION INFO (1994/95 PRICES)
Adult Standing: £6.00
Adult Seating: £8.00 - £10.00 (Members only)
Child Standing: £3.00 (Members only)
Child Seating: £5.00 (Wakeman Stand)
Away Standing: £6.00 (No concessions)
Away Seating: £10.00 (No concessions)
Programme Price: £1.00
FAX Number: (0743) 236384

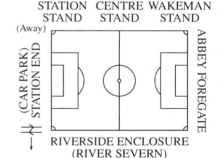

STATION CENTRE WAKEMAN
STAND STAND STAND
(Away)
(CAR PARK) STATION END
ABBEY FOREGATE
RIVERSIDE ENCLOSURE
(RIVER SEVERN)

Travelling Supporters Information:
Routes: From North: Take A49 or A53 then 2nd exit at roundabout into Telford Way (A5112). After 0.75 mile take 2nd exit at roundabout. Turn right at 'T' junction into Abbey Foregate for Ground; From South: Take A49 to Town Centre and at end of Coleham Head, turn right into Abbey Foregate; From East: Take A5 then A458 into Town Centre straight forward to Abbey Foregate; From West: Take A458 then A5 around Ring Road, Roman Road, then turn left into Hereford Road and at end of Coleman Head turn right into Abbey Foregate.

SOUTHAMPTON FC

Founded: 1885	**Record Attendance**: 31,044 (8/10/69)
Turned Professional: 1894	**Colours**: Shirts - Red & White
Limited Company: 1897	Shorts - Black
Admitted to League: 1920	**Telephone No.**: (0703) 220505
Former Name(s): Southampton St. Mary's	**Ticket Information**: (0703) 228575
YMCA FC (1885-1897)	**Pitch Size**: 110 × 72yds
Nickname: 'Saints'	**Ground Capacity**: 15,000
Ground: The Dell, Milton Road, Southampton	**Seating Capacity**: 15,000
SO9 4XX	

GENERAL INFORMATION
Supporters Club Administrator:
The Secretary
Address: Saints Supporters' Social Club,
The Dell, Milton Road, Southampton
Telephone Number: (0703) 336450
Car Parking: Street Parking
Coach Parking: By Police Direction
Nearest Railway Station: Southampton
Central (1 mile)
Nearest Bus Station: West Quay Road by
Centre 2000
Club Shop:
Opening Times: Monday-Saturday 9.00-5.00
(closed Wednesday)
Telephone No.: (0703) 236400
Postal Sales: Yes
Nearest Police Station: Civic Centre,
Southampton (1 mile)
Police Force: Hampshire
Police Telephone No.: (0703) 581111

GROUND INFORMATION
Away Supporters' Entrances: Archers Road
Turnstiles 16-20
Away Supporters' Sections: Upper/Lower East Stand
Archers Road End
Family Facilities: **Location of Stand**:
West Stand - Lower Seats
Capacity of Stand: 1,282

ADMISSION INFO (1994/95 PRICES)
Adult Seating: £11.00 - £14.00/£13.00 - £16.00
Child Seating: £5 or £6 - Lower East/West Stand Only
Programme Price: £1.50
FAX Number: (0703) 330360
Note: Matches are split into Categories of 'Silver' and
'Gold'. Prices shown to the left of the / are Silver

(Away)　EAST STAND

ARCHERS ROAD END

WILTON AVENUE / MILTON ROAD

Blind　　Wheelchairs

WEST STAND
HILL LANE/MILTON ROAD

Travelling Supporters Information:
Routes: From North: Take A33 into the Avenue and turn right into Northlands Road. Turn right at end into Archer's Road; From East: Take M27 to A334 and follow signs Southampton A3024. Then follow signs The West into Commercial Road, turn right into Hill Lane then 1st right into Milton Road; From West: Take A35 then A3024 following signs City Centre into Fourposts Hill then left into Hill Lane and 1st right into Milton Road.

SOUTHEND UNITED FC

Founded: 1906	**Record Attendance**: 31,033 (10/1/79)
Turned Professional: 1906	**Colours**: Shirts - Blue, Yellow and Red
Limited Company: 1919	Shorts - Blue, Yellow and Red
Admitted to League: 1920	**Telephone No.**: (0702) 340707
Former Name(s): Southend Athletic FC	**Ticket Information**: (0702) 435602
Nickname: 'Shrimpers' 'Blues'	**Pitch Size**: 110 × 74yds
Ground: Roots Hall Ground, Victoria Avenue,	**Ground Capacity**: 11,610
Southend-on-Sea SS2 6NQ	**Seating Capacity**: 11,610

GENERAL INFORMATION
Supporters Club Secretary: Tony Walters
Address: c/o Club
Telephone Number: (0702) 340707
Car Parking: Car Park at Ground (500 cars)
- Season Ticket Holders Only + Street Parking
Coach Parking: Car Park
Nearest Railway Station: Prittlewell (0.5 ml)
Nearest Bus Station: London Road,
Southend
Club Shop:
Opening Times: Weekdays & Matchdays
10.30-4.30pm (except Wednesdays)
Telephone No.: (0702) 435067 / 601351
Postal Sales: Yes
Nearest Police Station: Southend-on-Sea
(0.25 mile)
Police Force: Essex
Police Telephone No.: (0702) 431212

GROUND INFORMATION
Away Supporters' Entrances: North Stand Turnstiles
Away Supporters' Sections: North Stand (Open);
East Stand South Seats
Family Facilities: Location of Stand:
West Stand
Capacity of Stand: 3,019

ADMISSION INFO (1994/95 PRICES)
Adult Seating: £8.00 - £15.00
Child Seating: £4.50 Members
Away Seating: £8.00
Programme Price: £1.40
FAX Number: (0702) 330164

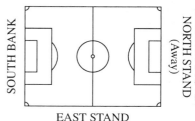

Travelling Supporters Information:
Routes: From North & West: Take A127 into Southend then at roundabout take 3rd exit into Victoria Avenue; From South: Take A13 following signs for Southend and turn left into West Road. At the end of West Road turn left into Victoria Avenue.

STOCKPORT COUNTY FC

Founded: 1883
Turned Professional: 1891
Limited Company: 1908
Admitted to League: 1900
Former Name(s): Heaton Norris Rovers FC; Heaton Norris FC
Nickname: 'Hatters' 'County'
Ground: Edgeley Park, Hardcastle Road, Edgeley, Stockport   SK3 9DD

Record Attendance: 27,833 (11/2/50)
Colours: Shirts - Blue with Red & Blue Flashes
Shorts - White
Telephone No.: (061) 480-8888
Ticket Information: (061) 480-8888
Pitch Size: 111 × 71yds
Ground Capacity: 9,720
Seating Capacity: 4,200

GENERAL INFORMATION
Supporters Club Administrator:
Simon Dawson
Address: c/o Club Shop
Telephone Number: (061) 480-8117
Car Parking: Street Parking
Coach Parking: By Police Direction
Nearest Railway Station: Stockport (5 minutes walk)
Nearest Bus Station: Mersey Square (10 minutes walk)
Club Shop: (061) 480-8117
Opening Times: Weekdays 9.00-5.00pm
Saturdays 9.30-12.30pm
Telephone No.: (061) 480-8117
Postal Sales: Yes
Nearest Police Station: Stockport (1 mile)
Police Force: Greater Manchester
Police Telephone No.: (061) 872-5050

GROUND INFORMATION
Away Supporters' Entrances: Cheadle End Turnstiles
Away Supporters' Sections: Cheadle End
Family Facilities: **Location of Stand**:
In front of Main Stand & Barlow Stand
Capacity of Stand: 1,800

ADMISSION INFO (1994/95 PRICES)
Adult Standing: £6.50 - £7.00
Adult Seating: £9.50
Child Standing: £4.00
Child Seating: £4.50 - £5.00   (£3.50 Jnr. Members)
Away Fans: All priced £7.00 (No concessions)
Programme Price: £1.30
FAX Number: (061) 480-0230

Travelling Supporters Information:
Routes: From North, South & West: Exit M63 junction 11 and join A560, following signs for Cheadle, after 0.25 mile turn right into Edgeley Road and in 1 mile turn right into Caroline Street for Ground; From East: Take A6 or A560 into Stockport Town Centre and turn left into Greek Street. Take 2nd exit into Mercian Way (from roundabout) then turn left into Caroline Street - Ground straight ahead.

STOKE CITY FC

Founded: 1863	**Record Attendance**: 51,380 (29/3/37)
Turned Professional: 1885	**Colours**: Shirts - Red & White Stripes
Limited Company: 1908	Shorts - White
Admitted to League: 1888 (Founder)	**Telephone No.**: (0782) 413511
Former Name(s): Stoke FC	**Ticket Information**: (0782) 413961
Nickname: 'Potters'	**Pitch Size**: 116 × 72yds
Ground: Victoria Ground, Boothen Old Road,	**Ground Capacity**: 25,084
Stoke-on-Trent ST4 4EG	**Seating Capacity**: 9,625

GENERAL INFORMATION
Supporters Club Administrator:
Nic Mansfield
Address: 11A Westland Street, Penkhull,
Stoke-on-Trent   ST4 7HE
Telephone Number: (0782) 744674
Car Parking: Car Park at Ground (2,000 cars)
Coach Parking: Whieldon Road
Nearest Railway Station: Stoke-on-Trent
(10 minutes walk)
Nearest Bus Station: Hanley (2 miles)
Club Shop:
Opening Times: Monday to Friday 9.30-5.00
Saturdays 9.30-12.00
Telephone No.: (0782) 747078
Postal Sales: Yes
Nearest Police Station: Stoke-on-Trent
(0.25 mile)
Police Force: Staffordshire
Police Telephone No.: (0782) 744644

GROUND INFORMATION
Away Supporters' Entrances: Butler Street
Turnstiles 47-49, Stoke End 33-35/41-46
Away Supporters' Sections: Butler Street Stand &
Block A Stoke End Paddock
Family Facilities: Location of Stand:
Stoke End Stand
Capacity of Stand: 2,000
ADMISSION INFO (1994/95 PRICES)
Adult Standing: £7.50
Adult Seating: £11.00
Child Standing: £5.00
Child Seating: £6.00
Programme Price: £1.50
FAX Number: (0782) 46422

(CAR PARK)
BUTLER STREET
(Away)

LONSDALE STREET

STOKE END

BOOTHEN END

BOOTHEN STAND
BOOTHEN OLD ROAD

Travelling Supporters Information:
Routes: From North, South & West: Exit M6 junction 15 and follow signs Stoke (A5006) and join A500.
Branch left 0.75 mile and take 2nd exit at roundabout into Campbell Road for Ground; From East: Take
A50 into Stoke Town Centre and turn left at crossroads into Lonsdale Street for Campbell Road.

Sunderland AFC

Founded: 1879
Turned Professional: 1886
Limited Company: 1906
Admitted to League: 1890
Former Name(s): Sunderland & District Teachers FC
Nickname: 'Rokerites'
Ground: Roker Park, Grantham Road, Roker Sunderland SR6 9SW

Record Attendance: 75,118 (8/3/33)
Colours: Shirts - Red & White Stripes
Shorts - Black
Telephone No.: (091) 514-0332
Ticket Information: (091) 514-0332
Pitch Size: 113 × 74yds
Ground Capacity: 22,657
Seating Capacity: 7,753

GENERAL INFORMATION
Supporters Club Administrator:
Audrey Baillie
Address: 36 Roker Baths Road, Roker, Sunderland
Telephone Number: (091) 567-0067
Car Parking: Car Park for 1,500 cars
Coach Parking: Seafront, Roker
Nearest Railway Station: Seaburn
Nearest Bus Station: Town Centre (2 miles)
Club Shop: Town Centre & Roker Park
Opening Times: Monday-Saturday 9.00-5.00
Telephone No.: (091) 564-0002
Postal Sales: Yes
Nearest Police Station: Southwick (1.25 ml)
Police Force: Northumbria
Police Telephone No.: (091) 510-2020

GROUND INFORMATION
Away Supporters' Entrances: Roker End Turnstiles
Away Supporters' Sections: Roker End
Family Facilities: **Location of Stand**: Centre Stand
Capacity of Stand: 514

ADMISSION INFO (1994/95 PRICES)
Adult Standing: £8.00 Members   £9 Non-members
Adult Seating: £11.00 - £13.00
Child Standing: £4.00
Child Seating: £11.00   (Family Enclosure £7.00)
Programme Price: £1.00
FAX Number: (091) 514-5854

ASSOCIATION ROAD
CLOCK STAND

ROKER BATHS ROAD
(Away) ROKER END

HAMPDEN ROAD
FULWELL END

MAIN STAND

ROKER WING   MAIN STAND   FULWELL WING

Travelling Supporters Information:
Routes: Take A19 to Sunderland. Take A1231 turn-off for Sunderland North and follow the signs to the City Centre. After 2 miles, at traffic lights, go straight ahead in the left lane marked A1289 to Roker. After 1 mile, follow the Roker A183 signs. 200 yards after that follow signs for Whitburn & Sea Front (A183) and after 0.5 mile turn left down side street, the football ground is straight ahead.

SWANSEA CITY FC

Founded: 1900	**Record Attendance**: 32,796 (17/2/68)
Turned Professional: 1912	**Colours**: Shirts - White
Limited Company: 1912	Shorts - White
Admitted to League: 1920	**Telephone No.**: (0792) 474114
Former Name(s): Swansea Town FC	**Ticket Information**: (0792) 474114
(1900-1970)	**Pitch Size**: 110 × 74yds
Nickname: 'Swans'	**Ground Capacity**: 16,499
Ground: Vetch Field, Swansea SA1 3SU	**Seating Capacity**: 3,414

GENERAL INFORMATION

Supporters Club Administrator: John Button
Address: 159 Western Street, Swansea
Telephone Number: (0792) 460958
Car Parking: Kingsway Car Park (200 yards) & Clarence Terrace Car Park (50 yards)
Coach Parking: By Police Direction
Nearest Railway Station: Swansea High Street (0.5 mile)
Nearest Bus Station: Quadrant Depot (0.25 mile)
Club Shop: 33 William Street, Swansea SA1 3QS
Opening Times: Weekdays 10.00-4.30 Matchdays 9.30-5.00
Telephone No.: (0792) 462584
Postal Sales: Yes
Nearest Police Station: Swansea Central (0.5 mile)
Police Force: South Wales
Police Telephone No.: (0792) 456999

GROUND INFORMATION

Away Supporters' Entrances: Richardson Street Turnstiles
Away Supporters' Sections: West Terrace Enclosure - Partially covered
Family Facilities: Location of Stand: Jewson Family Enclosure (West Side of Centre Stand)
Capacity of Stand: 321 seats

ADMISSION INFO (1994/95 PRICES)

Adult Standing: £6.50
Adult Seating: £8.50 - £9.00
Child Standing: £3.50
Child Seating: Family + 1 = £12.50   + 2 = £14.50
Programme Price: £1.20
FAX Number: (0792) 646120

MADOC STREET
NORTH BANK

RICHARDSON STREET

WEST TERRACE
(Away)

WILLIAM STREET
EAST STAND

CENTRE STAND
GLAMORGAN STREET

Travelling Supporters Information:
Routes: From All Parts: Exit M4 junction 45 and follow Swansea (A4067) signs into City Centre along High Street. Passing Railway Station into Castle Station then Wind Street and take 3rd exit at roundabout into Victoria Road and bear right towards bus station at Quadrant for Ground.

SWINDON TOWN FC

Founded: 1881	**Record Attendance**: 32,000 (15/1/72)
Turned Professional: 1895	**Colours**: Shirts - Red
Limited Company: 1897	Shorts - Red
Admitted to League: 1920	**Telephone No.**: (0793) 430430
Former Name(s): None	**Ticket Information**: (0793) 529000
Nickname: 'Robins'	**Pitch Size**: 114 × 74yds
Ground: County Ground, County Road,	**Ground Capacity**: 14,000 (Temporary)
Swindon SN1 2ED	**Seating Capacity**: 14,000 (Temporary)

GENERAL INFORMATION
Supporters Club Administrator:
Miss S.Cobern
Address: 31 Pewsham Road, Penhill,
Swindon
Telephone Number: (0793) 481061
Car Parking: Town Centre
Coach Parking: Car Park Adjacent
Nearest Railway Station: Swindon (0.5 mile)
Nearest Bus Station: Swindon (0.5 mile)
Club Shop: Robins Corner
Opening Times: Weekdays 9.00am - 5.00pm
Saturdays 9.00-3.00pm on matchdays only
Telephone No.: (0793) 430430
Postal Sales: Yes
Nearest Police Station: Fleming Way,
Swindon
Police Force: Wiltshire
Police Telephone No.: (0793) 528111

GROUND INFORMATION
Away Supporters' Entrances: Intel Stand
Away Supporters' Sections: Intel Stand
Family Facilities: **Location of Stand**:
Town End Stand
Capacity of Stand: 1,950

ADMISSION INFO (1994/95 PRICES)
Adult Seating: £10.00 - £14.00
Child Seating: £5.00 - £8.00
Programme Price: £1.50
FAX Number: (0793) 536170

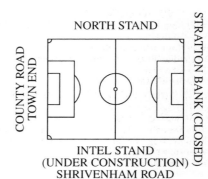

Travelling Supporters Information:
Routes: From London & East & South: Exit M4 junction 15 and take A345 into Swindon along Queen's Drive, take 3rd exit at 'Magic Roundabout' into County Road; From West: Exit M4 junction 15 then as above; From North: Take M4 or A345/A420/A361 to County Road roundabout then as above.

TORQUAY UNITED FC

Founded: 1898	**Record Attendance**: 21,908 (29/1/55)
Turned Professional: 1921	**Colours**: Shirts - Yellow, Navy & White Hoops
Limited Company: 1921	Shorts - Navy
Admitted to League: 1927	**Telephone No.**: (0803) 328666/7
Former Name(s): Torquay Town (1898-1910)	**Ticket Information**: (0803) 328666/7
Nickname: 'Gulls'	**Pitch Size**: 110 × 74yds
Ground: Plainmoor Ground, Torquay	**Ground Capacity**: 6,455
TQ1 3PS	**Seating Capacity**: 2,324

GENERAL INFORMATION
Supporters Club Chairman: Mr. T. Webb
Address: 50 Carlton Road, Torquay
Telephone Number: (0803) 297778
Car Parking: Street Parking
Coach Parking: Lymington Road Coach Station (0.5 mile)
Nearest Railway Station: Torquay (2 miles)
Nearest Bus Station: Lymington Road (0.5 mile)
Club Shop:
Opening Times: Matchdays & During Office Hours
Telephone No.: (0803) 328666
Postal Sales: Yes
Nearest Police Station: Torquay (1 mile)
Police Force: Devon & Cornwall
Police Telephone No.: (0803) 214491

GROUND INFORMATION
Away Supporters' Entrances: Babbacombe End Turnstiles
Away Supporters' Sections: Babbacombe End
Family Facilities: **Location of Stand**: Ellacombe End
Capacity of Stand: 1,370

ADMISSION INFO (1994/95 PRICES)
Adult Standing: £6.00
Adult Seating: £6.00
Child Standing: £3.00 (Away Standing/Seating
Child Seating: £3.00   No concessions)
Programme Price: £1.20
FAX Number: (0803) 323976

Travelling Supporters Information:
Routes: From North & East: Take M5 to A38 and A380 to Kingskerwell. Take 1st exit at roundabout (1 mile) and in 1 mile turn left following Babbacombe (A3022) signs. Turn left (0.75 mile) into Westhill Road for Warbro Road; From West: Take A380 into Town Centre and follow signs Teignmouth (A379) to Lymington Road. Turn right into Upton Hill and follow into Bronshill Road. Take 2nd left into Derwent Road and at end turn right and right again into Marnham Road.

TOTTENHAM HOTSPUR FC

Founded: 1882	**Record Attendance**: 75,038 (5/3/38)
Turned Professional: 1895	**Colours**: Shirts - White
Limited Company: 1898	Shorts - Navy Blue
Admitted to League: 1908	**Telephone No.**: (081) 365-5000
Former Name(s): Hotspur FC (1882-85)	**Ticket Office**: (081) 365-5050
Nickname: 'Spurs'	**Pitch Size**: 110 × 73yds
Ground: White Hart Lane, 748 High Road,	**Ground Capacity**: 24,600
Tottenham, London N17 0AP	**Seating Capacity**: 24,600

GENERAL INFORMATION
Supporters Club Administrator:
Linda Watkins
Address: Spurs Members Club, 752B High Road, Tottenham N17
Telephone Number: (081) 365-5150
Car Parking: None within 0.25 mile
Coach Parking: Northumberland Park Coach Park
Nearest Railway Station: White Hart Lane (Nearby)/Northumberland Park
Nearest Tube Station: Seven Sisters (Victoria); Manor House (Piccadilly)
Club Shop:
Opening Times: Weekdays 9.30-5.30 and Matchdays 9.30-6.00
Telephone No.: (081) 365-5042
Postal Sales: Yes
Nearest Police Station: Tottenham (1 mile)
Police Force: Metropolitan
Police Telephone No.: (081) 801-3443

GROUND INFORMATION
Away Supporters' Entrances: Park Lane
Away Supporters' Sections: South Stand, Park Lane
Family Facilities: Location of Stand:
Members Stand
Capacity of Stand: 6,905

ADMISSION INFO (1994/95 PRICES)
Adult Seating: £13 - £30   (Members £12 - £17)
Child Seating: Members Only £6.00 - £8.50
Programme Price: £1.50
FAX Number: (081) 365-5005

WORCESTER AVENUE
EAST STAND

PAXTON ROAD
NORTH STAND
(Members Only)

PARK LANE
SOUTH STAND
(Away)

WEST STAND
HIGH ROAD

Travelling Supporters Information:
Routes: From All Parts: Take A406 North Circular to Edmonton and at traffic lights follow signs for Tottenham (A1010) into Fore Street for Ground.

TRANMERE ROVERS FC

Founded: 1881	**Record Attendance**: 24,424 (5/2/72)
Turned Professional: 1912	**Colours**: Shirts - White
Limited Company: 1920	Shorts - White
Admitted to League: 1921	**Telephone No.**: (051) 608-3677
Former Name(s): Belmont FC	**Ticket Information**: (051) 608-3677
Nickname: 'Rovers'	**Pitch Size**: 112 × 74yds
Ground: Prenton Park, Prenton Road West,	**Ground Capacity**: 17,000 (January 1995)
Birkenhead L42 9PN	**Seating Capacity**: 17,000 (January 1995)

GENERAL INFORMATION

Supporters Club Administrator: A. Price
Address: c/o Club
Telephone Number: (051) 608-3677
Car Parking: Large Car Park at Ground
Coach Parking: At Ground
Nearest Railway Station: Hamilton Square, Rock Ferry (1 mile)
Nearest Bus Station: Birkenhead
Club Shop:
Opening Times: Weekdays & Matchdays 9.00-5.00
Telephone No.: (051) 608-0438
Postal Sales: Yes
Nearest Police Station: Bebington (2 miles)
Police Force: Merseyside
Police Telephone No.: (051) 709-6010

GROUND INFORMATION

Away Supporters' Entrances: Bebington End Turnstiles - access from Main Car Park
Away Supporters' Sections: Bebington End (open)
Family Facilities: **Location of Stand**:
Family Enclosure
Capacity of Stand: 3,800

ADMISSION INFO (1994/95 PRICES)

Adult Seating: £7.50-£10.00
Child Seating: £5.00-£10.00
Programme Price: £1.20
FAX Number: (051) 608-4385
Family Stand: £9.00 Adult ; £5.00 Children (seated)

FAMILY
ENCLOSURE   CAR PARK
(Disabled)   MAIN STAND

BEBINGTON KOP END
(Away)

PRENTON PARK WEST
TOWN END

BOROUGH ROAD SIDE

Note: Three sides of the ground are being redeveloped and stand names may change.

Travelling Supporters Information:
Routes: From North: Take Mersey Tunnel to M53, exit junction 3 and take 1st exit at roundabout (A552), in 1.25 mile turn right at crossroads (B5151) then left into Prenton Road West; From South & East: Exit M53 junction 4 and take 4th exit at roundabout (B5151). After 2.5 miles turn right into Prenton Road West.

WALSALL FC

Founded: 1888	**Record Attendance**: 10,628 (20/5/91)
Turned Professional: 1888	(England B vs. Switzerland)
Limited Company: 1921	**Colours**: Shirts - Red & White Stripes
Admitted to League: 1892	Shorts - Black
Former Name(s): Walsall Town Swifts FC	**Telephone No.**: (0922) 22791
(1888-95)	**Ticket Information**: (0922) 22791
Nickname: 'Saddlers'	**Pitch Size**: 110 × 73yds
Ground: Bescot Stadium, Bescot Crescent,	**Ground Capacity**: 9,485
Walsall, West Midlands WS1 4SA	**Seating Capacity**: 6,685

GENERAL INFORMATION
Supporters Club Administrator:
John Wilson
Address: Saddlers Club, Wallows Lane,
Walsall
Telephone Number: (0922) 22257
Car Parking: Car Park at Ground
Coach Parking: At Ground
Nearest Railway Station: Bescot (Adjacent)
Nearest Bus Station: Bradford Place, Walsall
Bus Services to Ground: 2/312/323/636/637
Specials : 977/978/979/980/981
Club Shop:
Opening Times: Weekdays 10.00-2.00pm
and Matchdays 9.30-5.15pm
Telephone No.: (0922) 643331
Postal Sales: Yes
Nearest Police Station: Walsall (2 miles)
Police Force: West Midlands
Police Telephone No.: (0922) 38111

GROUND INFORMATION
Away Supporters' Entrances: Highgate Stand
Turnstiles 1-4
Away Supporters' Sections: Highgate Stand
Family Facilities: **Location of Stand**:
In front of Highgate Stand - Blocks A & B
Capacity of Stand: 800 Seats

ADMISSION INFO (1994/95 PRICES)
Adult Standing: £6.50
Adult Seating: £8.00 - £9.00
Child Standing: £5.00
Child Seating: £5.00 - £9.00
Programme Price: £1.20
FAX Number: (0922) 613202

HIGHGATE STAND
(Away)

GILBERT ALSO STAND

(BESCOT CRESCENT)
WILLIAM SHARP STAND

H.L. FELLOWS STAND

Travelling Supporters Information:
Routes: From All Parts: Exit M6 junction 9 turning North towards Walsall onto the A461. After 0.25 mile turn right into Wallows Lane and pass over Railway Bridge. Then take 1st right into Bescot Crescent and ground is 0.5 mile along on left adjacent to Bescot Railway Station.

WATFORD FC

Founded: 1891
Turned Professional: 1897
Limited Company: 1909
Admitted to League: 1920
Former Name(s): Formed by Amalgamation of West Herts FC & St Mary's FC
Nickname: 'Hornets'
Ground: Vicarage Road Stadium, Watford WD1 8ER

Record Attendance: 34,099 (3/2/69)
Colours: Shirts - Yellow with Black & Red Shorts - Black
Telephone No.: (0923) 230933
Ticket Information: (0923) 220393
Pitch Size: 115 × 75yds
Ground Capacity: 16,000 (approximately)
Seating Capacity: 16,000 (approximately)

GENERAL INFORMATION
Supporters Club Administrator:
c/o Marketing Department
Address: c/o Club
Telephone Number: (0923) 225761
Car Parking: Nearby Multi-Storey Car Park
Coach Parking: Cardiff Road Car Park
Nearest Railway Station: Station at Ground (for Big Games only) or Watford Junction
Nearest Bus Station: Watford
Club Shop:
Opening Times: Monday to Saturday 9.00-5.00
Telephone No.: (0923) 220847
Postal Sales: Yes
Nearest Police Station: Shady Lane, Clarendon Road, Watford (1.5 miles)
Police Force: Hertfordshire
Police Telephone No.: (0923) 244444

GROUND INFORMATION
Away Supporters' Entrances: Rous Stand Entrance, Vicarage Road
Away Supporters' Sections: Rous Stand Lower Tier
Family Facilities: **Location of Stand**: Family Block (Season Ticket holders only)
Capacity of Stand: 750 Seated in Family Block

ADMISSION INFO (1994/95 PRICES)
Adult Seating: £9.00 or £11.50
Child Seating: £6.00 or £11.50
Programme Price: £1.50
FAX Number: (0923) 239759

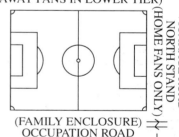

ROUS STAND
(AWAY FANS IN LOWER TIER)

SOUTH STAND
(UNDER CONSTRUCTION)

VICARAGE ROAD
NORTH STAND
(HOME FANS ONLY)

(FAMILY ENCLOSURE)
OCCUPATION ROAD
EAST STAND

Travelling Supporters Information:
Routes: From North: Exit M1 junction 5 take 2nd exit at roundabout, A41 signposted Harrow. Take 3rd exit at next roundabout to Hartspring Lane. Follow through traffic lights and continue straight ahead (now Aldenham Road) to next roundabout. Take 2nd exit still following Aldenham Road, to next traffic lights. When through lights, move into right-hand lane (marked Watford) and follow one-way around to Bushey Station, then moving into left-hand lane. Turn left under Bushey Arches, into Eastbury Road. At traffic lights turn right into Deacons Hill and continue to next traffic lights, turning left into Cardiff Road for visitors' entrance to stadium/coach park. Straight on for limited off-street parking or car parks in shopping centre; From South: Exit M1 junction 5 take first exit off roundabout, A41 signposted Harrow (then as North); From East: Exit M25 at junction 21A, join the M1 at junction 6. Exit Junction 5 (then as North); From West: Exit M25 junction 19, take 3rd exit at roundabout, A411 (Hempstead Road), signposted Watford. After 2 miles go straight on at roundabout then at next roundabout take 3rd exit, Rickmansworth Road. Take second turning on left into Cassio Road. Through traffic lights, to Merton Road, then Wiggenhall Road. At traffic lights, turn right into Cardiff Road (then as North).

WEST BROMWICH ALBION FC

Founded: 1879
Turned Professional: 1885
Limited Company: 1892
Admitted to League: 1888 (Founder)
Former Name(s): West Bromwich Strollers (1879-1880)
Nickname: 'Throstles' 'Baggies' 'Albion'
Ground: The Hawthorns, Halfords Lane, West Bromwich, West Midlands B71 4LF

Record Attendance: 64,815 (6/3/37)
Colours: Shirts - Navy Blue & White Stripes
Shorts - White
Telephone No.: (021) 525-8888
Ticket Information: (021) 553-5472
Pitch Size: 115 × 75yds
Ground Capacity: 18,000 (26,000 December)
Seating Capacity: 18,000 (26,000 December)

GENERAL INFORMATION
Supporters Club Administrator:
Alan Cleverley
Address: 1 St. Christophers, Hamstead Hill, Handsworth Wood, Birmingham B20 1BP
Telephone Number: (021) 551-6439
Car Parking: Halfords Lane Car Parks, W.B.B.S. Stand Car Park
Coach Parking: W.B.B.S. Stand Car Park
Nearest Railway Station: Rolfe Street, Smethwick (1.5 miles), Hawthorns (200yds)
Nearest Bus Station: Town Centre
Bus Services to Ground: 74/78/79/450
Club Shop:
Opening Times: Weekdays 9.00-5.00
Saturday Matchdays 9.00-2.45
Telephone No.: (021) 525-2145
Postal Sales: Yes
Nearest Police Station: Holyhead Road, Handsworth (0.5 mile)
Police Force: West Midlands
Police Telephone No.: (021) 554-3414

GROUND INFORMATION
Away Supporters' Entrances: Smethwick End Turnstiles (P-block)
Away Supporters' Sections: Smethwick End (Covered Seating)
Family Facilities: **Location of Stand**:
West Bromwich Building Society Family Stand (Home supporters only)
Capacity of Stand: 5,200

ADMISSION INFO (1994/95 PRICES)
Adult Seating: £8.00 or £11.00
Child Seating: £4.00 or £6.00
Programme Price: £1.20
FAX Number: (021) 553-6634

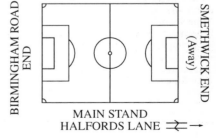

WEST BROMWICH BUILDING SOCIETY FAMILY STAND

BIRMINGHAM ROAD END

SMETHWICK END (Away)

MAIN STAND
HALFORDS LANE

Travelling Supporters Information:
Routes: From All Parts: Exit M5 junction 1 and take Birmingham Road (A41) for Ground.

WEST HAM UNITED FC

Founded: 1895	**Record Attendance**: 42,322 (17/10/70)
Turned Professional: 1900	**Colours**: Shirts - Claret & Blue
Limited Company: 1900	Shorts - White
Admitted to League: 1919	**Telephone No.**: (081) 548-2748
Former Name(s): Thames Iron Works F.C.	**Ticket Information**: (081) 472-3322
Nickname: 'Hammers'	**Pitch Size**: 112 × 72yds
Ground: Boleyn Ground, Green Street,	**Ground Capacity**: 20,024 (25,634 from
Upton Park, London E13 9AZ	**Seating Capacity**: 20,024 January 1995)

GENERAL INFORMATION
Supporters Club Administrator:
Mr. T. Jenkinson
Address: West Ham Supporters' Club,
Castle Street, East Ham, London   E6 1PP
Telephone Number: (081) 472-1680
Car Parking: Street Parking
Coach Parking: By Police Direction
Nearest Railway Station: Barking
Nearest Tube Station: Upton Park (5 mins.)
Club Shop: The Hammers Shop
Opening Times: Weekdays & Matchdays
9.30-5.00
Telephone No.: (081) 548-2722
Postal Sales: Yes
Nearest Police Station: East Ham High Street
South (0.5 mile)
Police Force: Metropolitan
Police Telephone No.: (081) 593-8232

GROUND INFORMATION
Away Supporters' Entrances: Turnstiles 23-29,
Castle Street
Away Supporters' Sections: Bobby Moore Stand
Family Facilities: **Location of Stand**:
East Stand Side
Capacity of Stand: 806

ADMISSION INFO (1994/95 PRICES)
Adult Seating: £11.00 - £18.00
Child Seating: No concessions   (reductions in
Programme Price: £1.50   Family Area)
FAX Number: (081) 471-2997

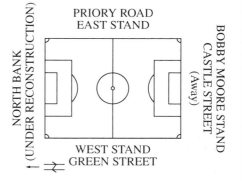

Travelling Supporters Information:
Routes: From North & West: Take North Circular (A406) to A124 (East Ham) then along Barking Road for approximately 1.5 miles until approaching traffic lights at crossroad. Turn right into Green Street, ground is on right-hand side; From South: Take Blackwall Tunnel and A13 to Canning Town. Follow signs for East Ham (A124). After 1.75 miles turn left into Green Street; From East: Take A13 and turn right onto A117 at crossroads. After approximately 1 mile turn left at crossroads onto A124. Turn right (0.75 mile) into Green Street.

WIGAN ATHLETIC AFC

Founded: 1932
Turned Professional: 1932
Limited Company: 1986
Admitted to League: 1978
Former Name(s): None
Nickname: 'Latics'
Ground: Springfield Park, Wigan, Lancs.
WN6 7BA

Record Attendance: 27,500 (12/12/51)
Colours: Shirts - Blue & Black Stripes
Shorts - Black with Blue Trim
Telephone No.: (0942) 44433
Ticket Information: (0942) 44433
Pitch Size: 117 × 73yds
Ground Capacity: 5,500
Seating Capacity: 900

GENERAL INFORMATION
Supporters Club Administrator: Joe Mills
Address: c/o Club
Telephone Number: (0942) 43512
Car Parking: Street Parking
Coach Parking: Shevington End
Nearest Railway Station: Wallgate & North West (1 mile)
Nearest Bus Station: Wigan
Club Shop:
Opening Times: Weekdays & Matchdays 9.00-5.00
Telephone No.: (0942) 44433
Postal Sales: Yes
Nearest Police Station: Harrogate Street, Wigan (1 mile)
Police Force: Greater Manchester
Police Telephone No.: (0942) 44981

GROUND INFORMATION
Away Supporters' Entrances: Shevington End Turnstiles
Away Supporters' Sections: Shevington End (Partially covered)
Family Facilities: **Location of Stand**:
In front of Phoenix Stand (Heinz Family Enclosure)
Capacity of Stand: 128

ADMISSION INFO (1994/95 PRICES)
Adult Standing: £6.50
Adult Seating: £8.00
Child Standing: £4.00
Child Seating: £6.00
Programme Price: £1.50
FAX Number: (0942) 494654

HEINZ FAMILY ENCLOSURE (Disabled)   PHOENIX STAND

SHEVINGTON ROAD TOWN END

SHEVINGTON ROAD (Away)

POPULAR SIDE
ST. ANDREWS DRIVE

Travelling Supporters Information:
Routes: From North: Exit M6 junction 27 following signs for Wigan (A5209), turn right (0.25 mile) (B5206). Turn left 1 mile and in 4.5 miles take left into Springfield Road; From South: Exit M6 junction 25 following signs for Wigan (A49). Turn left into Robin Park Road and into Scot Lane. Turn right at 3rd traffic lights into Woodhouse Lane and left at traffic lights into Springfield Road; From East: Take A557 into Town Centre then left into Robin Park Road (then as South).

WIMBLEDON FC

Founded: 1889
Turned Professional: 1964
Limited Company: 1964
Admitted to League: 1977
Former Name(s): Wimbledon Old Centrals
FC (1889-1905)
Nickname: 'Dons'
Ground: Selhurst Park, London   SE25 6PY

Record Attendance: 30,115 (1992-93)
Colours: Shirts - Blue
               Shorts - Blue
Telephone No.: (081) 771-2233
Ticket Information: (081) 771-8841
Pitch Size: 110 × 74yds
Ground Capacity: 18,103
Seating Capacity: 18,103

GENERAL INFORMATION
Supporters Club Administrator:
Sue Moody
Address: c/o Club
Telephone Number: (081) 771-2233
Car Parking: Street Parking
Coach Parking: Thornton Heath
Nearest Railway Station: Selhurst/Norwood
Junction/Thornton Heath
Club Shop:
Opening Times: Weekdays & Matchdays
9.30-5.30
Telephone No.: (081) 653-5584
Postal Sales: Yes
Nearest Police Station: South Norwood
(15 minutes walk)
Police Force: Metropolitan
Police Telephone No.: (081) 653-8568

GROUND INFORMATION
Away Supporters' Entrances: Park Road
Away Supporters' Sections: Corner - Park Road
(Covered Seating)
Family Facilities: **Location of Stand**:
Members Stand (Clifton Road End)
Capacity of Stand: -

ADMISSION INFO (1994/95 PRICES)
Adult Seating: £4.00 - £22.00
Child Seating: £4.00 - £11.00
Programme Price: £1.50
FAX Number: (081) 768-0640

PARK ROAD
ARTHUR WAIT STAND
ARTHUR WAIT ENCLOSURE
(Away)

WHITEHORSE LANE STAND

HOLMESDALE ROAD
(CLOSED)

MAIN STAND
CLIFTON ROAD

Travelling Supporters Information:
Routes: From North: Take M1/A1 to North Circular (A406) to Chiswick. Take South Circular (A205) to Wandsworth, take A3 to A214 and follow signs to Streatham to A23. Turn left onto B273 (1 mile), follow to end and turn left into High Street and into Whitehorse Lane; From East: Take A232 (Croydon Road) to Shirley and join A215 (Norwood Road), after 2.25 miles take left into Whitehorse Lane; From South: Take A23 and follow signs Crystal Palace B266 through Thornton Heath into Whitehorse Lane; From West: Take M4 to Chiswick (then as North).

WOLVERHAMPTON WANDERERS FC

Founded: 1877	**Record Attendance**: 61,315 (11/2/39)
Turned Professional: 1888	**Colours**: Shirts - Gold
Limited Company: 1892	Shorts - Black
Admitted to League: 1888 (Founder)	**Telephone No.**: (0902) 655000
Former Name(s): St. Luke's FC & The	**Ticket Information**: (0902) 653653
Wanderers FC (combined 1880)	**Pitch Size**: 116 × 74yds
Nickname: 'Wolves'	**Ground Capacity**: 28,500
Ground: Molineux Ground, Waterloo Road,	**Seating Capacity**: 28,500
Wolverhampton WV1 4QR	

Photo by John Sambrooks

GENERAL INFORMATION
Supporters Club Administrator:
Albert Bates
Address: 341 Penn Road, Penn,
Wolverhampton
Telephone Number: (0902) 330322
Car Parking: Around West Park & Rear of
Stan Cullis Stand
Coach Parking: By Police Direction
Nearest Railway Station: Wolverhamp.(1ml)
Nearest Bus Station: Wolverhamp. (0.25ml)
Bus Services to Ground: 3/503/503A/504/
505/506/507/531A/534/535/536/525/525A/682
Club Shop:
Opening Times: Weekdays & Matchdays
9.00-5.00
Telephone No.: (0902) 658777
Postal Sales: Yes
Nearest Police Station: Dunstall Road
(500 yds)
Police Force: West Midlands
Police Telephone No.: (0902) 649000

GROUND INFORMATION
Away Supporters' Entrances: Jack Harris Stand
Turnstiles Block 5
Away Supporters' Sections: Jack Harris Lower Tier
Block 5
Family Facilities: **Location of Stand**:
Billy Wright Stand - Lower Tier
Capacity of Stand: 2,500
ADMISSION INFO (1994/95 PRICES)
Adult Seating: £8.00 - £12.00
Child Seating: £6.00 - £8.00
Programme Price: £1.50
FAX Number: (0902) 647003

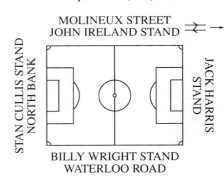

MOLINEUX STREET
JOHN IRELAND STAND

STAN CULLIS STAND
NORTH BANK

JACK HARRIS STAND

BILLY WRIGHT STAND
WATERLOO ROAD

Travelling Supporters Information:
Routes: From North: Exit M6 junction 12 following signs for Wolverhampton A5, then A449 and at roundabout take 2nd exit into Waterloo Road then turn left into Molineux Street; From South: Exit M5 junction 2 following signs for Wolverhampton A4123, turn right, then left into Ring Road, turn left (1 mile) into Waterloo Road, then turn right into Molineux Street; from East: Exit M6 junction 10 following signs Wolverhampton A454, turn right at crossroads into Stratford Street then turn left (0.25 mile) into Ring Road, right at crossroads into Waterloo Road then right into Molineux Street; From West: Take A454 and at roundabout turn left into Ring Road (then as East).

WREXHAM FC

Founded: 1873	**Record Attendance**: 34,445 (26/1/57)
Turned Professional: 1912	**Colours**: Shirts - Red
Limited Company: 1912	Shorts - White
Admitted to League: 1921	**Telephone No.**: (0978) 262129
Former Name(s): None	**Ticket Information**: (0978) 262129
Nickname: 'Robins'	**Pitch Size**: 111 × 71yds
Ground: Racecourse Ground, Mold Road,	**Ground Capacity**: 11,500
Wrexham, Clwyd	**Seating Capacity**: 5,026

GENERAL INFORMATION
Supporters Club Administrator:
Miss Ena Williams
Address: c/o Club
Telephone Number: (0978) 262129
Car Parking: Town Car Parks Nearby
Coach Parking: -
Nearest Railway Station: Wrexham
General (Adjacent)
Nearest Bus Station: Wrexham (King Street)
Club Shop: Promotions Office
Opening Times: Office Hours
Telephone No.: (0978) 352536
Postal Sales: Yes
Nearest Police Station: Bodhyfryd (HQ)
(1 mile)
Police Force: Wrexham Division
Police Telephone No.: (0978) 290222

GROUND INFORMATION
Away Supporters' Entrances: Mold End Turnstiles
Away Supporters' Sections: Marstons Stand, Mold
End (Covered)
Family Facilities: Location of Stand:
Yale Stand Town End
Capacity of Stand: 280

ADMISSION INFO (1994/95 PRICES)
Adult Standing: £6.50
Adult Seating: £8.50 or £9.00
Child Standing: £4.50
Child Seating: £6.50
Programme Price: £1.20
FAX Number: (0978) 357821

(CAR PARK)
YALE STAND

MARSTONS STAND
MOLD END
(Away)

CRISPIN LANE
KOP TOWN END

MOLD ROAD STAND ⇥→

Travelling Supporters Information:
Routes: From North & West: Take A483 and Wrexham Bypass to junction with A541. Branch left and at roundabout follow Wrexham signs into Mold Road; From South & East: Take A525 or A534 into Wrexham then follow A541 signs into Mold Road.

WYCOMBE WANDERERS

Founded: 1884
Former Name(s): None
Nickname: 'The Blues' & 'The Chairboys'
Ground: Adams Park, Hillbottom Road, Sands, High Wycombe, Bucks
Record Attendance: 7,802 (8/1/94) vs Norwich City

Colours: Shirts - Dark/Light Blue Quarters Shorts - Navy Blue
Telephone No.: (0494) 472100
Ticket Information: (0494) 472100
Pitch Size: 115 × 75yds
Ground Capacity: 8,500
Seating Capacity: 1,267

GENERAL INFORMATION
Supporters Club Administrator: None
Address: -
Telephone Number: -
Car Parking: Car Park at Ground (320 cars)
Coach Parking: Car Park at Ground
Nearest Railway Station: High Wycombe
Nearest Bus Station: High Wycombe
Club Shop: At Ground and also in Town
Opening Times: Weekdays & Matchdays
Telephone No.: (0494) 472100
Postal Sales: Yes
Nearest Police Station: Queen Victoria Road, High Wycombe (2.5 miles)
Police Force: Thames Valley
Police Telephone No.: (0494) 465888

GROUND INFORMATION
Away Supporters' Entrances: Hillbottom Road End
Away Supporters' Sections: Hillbottom Terrace
Family Facilities: Location of Stand: Family Section of Main Stand
Capacity of Family Stand: 180

ADMISSION INFO (1994/95 PRICES)
Adult Standing: £6.50
Adult Seating: £9.00
Child Standing: £4.00
Child Seating: £4.00 (Family Stand)
Programme Price: £1.20
FAX Number: (0494) 527633

MAIN STAND
PITCHSIDE ENCLOSURE

BUCKS FREE PRESS STAND

(AMERSHAM & WYCOMBE COLLEGE END)
HILLBOTTOM ROAD END
(Away)

DAVENPORT VERNON STAND

Travelling Supporters Information:
Routes: Exit M40 junction 4 and take A4010 road following Aylesbury signs. Go straight on at 3 mini-roundabouts and bear sharp left at 4th roundabout into Lane End Road. Fork right into Hillbottom Road at next roundabout. Ground at end. Hillbottom Road on Sands Industrial Estate; From Town Centre: Take A40 West, after 1.5 miles turn left into Chapel Lane (after traffic lights). Turn right then right again at mini-roundabout into Lane End Road - then as above.

YORK CITY FC

Founded: 1922	**Record Attendance**: 28,123 (5/3/38)
Turned Professional: 1922	**Colours**: Shirts - Red
Limited Company: 1922	Shorts - Blue
Admitted to League: 1929	**Telephone No.**: (0904) 624447
Former Name(s): None	**Ticket Information**: (0904) 624447
Nickname: 'Minstermen'	**Pitch Size**: 115 × 74yds
Ground: Bootham Crescent, York YO3 7AQ	**Ground Capacity**: 10,595
	Seating Capacity: 3,248

GENERAL INFORMATION
Supporters Club Administrator:
Raymond Wynn
Address: 155 Manor Drive North, York
Telephone Number: (0904) 797578
Car Parking: Street Parking
Coach Parking: By Police Direction
Nearest Railway Station: York (1 mile)
Nearest Bus Station: York
Club Shop:
Opening Times: Monday to Wednesday
9.00-5.00; Thursday 9.00-1.00; Friday 9.00-
3.00; Saturday Matches 1.00-3.00 + 4.40-5.30
Telephone No.: (0904) 645941
Postal Sales: Yes
Nearest Police Station: Fulford
Police Force: North Yorkshire
Police Telephone No.: (0904) 631321

GROUND INFORMATION
Away Supporters' Entrances: Grosvenor Road
Turnstiles
Away Supporters' Sections: Grosvenor Road End,
Bootham Crescent
Family Facilities: **Location of Stand**:
In front of Main Stand
Capacity of Stand: 164

ADMISSION INFO (1994/95 PRICES)
Adult Standing: £7.00
Adult Seating: £7.00 or £10.00
Child Standing: £4.00 (Members Only)
Child Seating: £4.00 - £6.00 (Members Only)
Programme Price: £1.20
FAX Number: (0904) 631457

POPULAR STAND

BOOTHAM CRESCENT
GROSVENOR ROAD END
(Away)

SHIPTON STREET

MAIN STAND

Travelling Supporters Information:
Routes: From North: Take A1 then A59 following York signs. Cross Railway Bridge and turn left (2 miles) into Water End. Turn right at end following City Centre signs for nearly 0.5 mile then turn left into Bootham Crescent; From South: Take A64 and turn left after Buckles Inn on to Outer Ring Road. Turn right onto A19 following City Centre signs for 1.5 miles then turn left into Bootham Crescent; From East: Take Outer Ring Road turning left onto A19 then as South; From West: Take Outer Ring Road turning right on to A19, then as South.

THE F.A. CARLING PREMIERSHIP

and

THE ENDSLEIGH INSURANCE FOOTBALL LEAGUE

STATISTICS

1993-1994

F.A. Premiership Season 1993/94

	ARSENAL	ASTON VILLA	BLACKBURN R.	CHELSEA	COVENTRY C.	EVERTON	IPSWICH TOWN	LEEDS UNITED	LIVERPOOL	MAN. CITY	MAN. UNITED	NEWCASTLE U.	NORWICH C.	OLDHAM ATH.	Q.P.R.	SHEFF. UTD.	SHEFF. WED.	SOUTHAMPTON	SWINDON T.	SPURS	WEST HAM	WIMBLEDON
ARSENAL		1-2	1-0	1-0	0-3	2-0	4-0	2-1	1-0	0-0	2-2	2-1	0-0	1-1	0-0	3-0	1-0	1-0	1-1	1-1	0-2	1-1
ASTON VILLA	1-2		0-1	1-0	0-0	0-0	0-1	1-0	2-1	0-0	1-2	0-2	0-0	1-2	4-1	1-0	2-2	0-2	5-0	1-0	3-1	0-1
BLACK. RVRS.	1-1	1-0		2-0	2-1	2-0	0-0	2-1	2-0	2-0	2-0	1-0	2-3	1-0	1-1	0-0	1-1	2-0	3-1	1-0	0-2	3-0
CHELSEA	0-2	1-1	1-2		1-2	4-2	1-1	1-1	1-0	0-0	1-0	1-0	1-2	0-1	2-0	3-2	1-1	2-0	2-0	4-3	2-0	2-0
COVENTRY CITY	1-0	0-1	2-1	1-1		2-1	1-0	0-2	1-0	4-0	0-1	2-1	2-1	1-1	0-1	0-0	1-1	1-1	1-1	1-0	1-1	1-2
EVERTON	1-1	0-1	0-3	4-2	0-0		0-0	1-1	2-0	1-0	0-1	0-2	1-5	2-1	0-3	4-2	0-2	1-0	6-2	0-1	0-1	3-2
IPSWICH TOWN	1-5	1-2	1-0	1-0	0-2	0-2		0-0	1-2	2-2	1-2	1-1	2-1	0-0	1-3	3-2	1-4	1-0	1-1	2-2	1-1	0-0
LEEDS UNITED	2-1	2-0	3-3	4-1	1-0	3-0	0-0		2-0	3-2	0-2	1-1	0-4	1-0	1-1	2-1	2-2	0-0	3-0	2-0	1-0	4-0
LIVERPOOL	0-0	2-1	0-1	2-1	1-0	2-1	1-0	2-0		2-1	3-3	0-2	0-1	2-1	3-2	1-2	2-0	4-2	2-2	1-2	2-0	1-1
MAN. CITY	0-0	3-0	0-2	2-2	1-1	1-0	2-1	1-1	1-1		2-3	2-1	1-1	1-1	3-0	0-0	1-3	1-1	2-1	0-2	0-0	0-1
MAN. UNITED	1-0	3-1	1-1	0-1	0-0	1-0	0-0	0-0	1-0	2-0		1-1	2-2	3-2	2-1	3-0	5-0	2-0	4-2	2-1	3-0	3-1
NEWCASTLE U.	2-0	5-1	1-1	0-0	4-0	1-0	2-0	1-1	3-0	2-0	1-1		3-0	3-2	1-2	4-0	4-2	1-2	7-1	0-1	2-0	4-0
NORWICH CITY	1-1	1-2	2-2	1-1	1-0	3-0	1-0	2-1	2-2	1-1	0-2	1-2		1-1	3-4	0-1	1-1	4-5	0-0	1-2	0-0	0-1
OLDHAM ATH.	0-0	1-1	1-2	2-1	3-3	0-1	0-3	1-1	0-3	0-0	2-5	1-3	2-1		4-1	1-1	0-0	2-1	2-1	0-2	1-2	1-1
Q.P.R.	1-1	2-2	1-0	1-1	5-1	2-1	3-0	0-4	1-3	1-1	2-3	1-2	2-2	2-0		2-1	1-2	2-1	1-3	1-1	0-0	1-0
SHEFF. UTD.	1-1	1-2	1-2	1-0	0-0	0-0	1-1	2-2	0-0	0-1	0-3	2-0	1-2	2-1	1-1		1-1	0-0	3-1	2-2	3-2	2-1
SHEFF. WED.	0-1	0-0	1-2	3-1	0-0	5-1	5-0	3-3	3-1	1-1	2-3	0-1	3-3	3-0	3-1	3-1		2-0	3-3	1-0	5-0	2-2
SOUTHAMPTON	0-4	4-1	3-1	3-1	1-0	0-2	0-1	0-2	4-2	0-1	1-3	2-1	0-1	1-3	0-1	3-3	1-1		5-1	1-0	0-2	1-0
SWINDON TOWN	0-4	1-2	1-3	1-3	3-1	1-1	2-2	0-5	0-5	1-3	2-2	2-2	3-3	0-1	1-0	0-0	0-1	2-1		2-1	1-1	2-4
TOTT. HOTSPUR	0-1	1-1	0-2	1-1	1-2	3-2	1-1	1-1	3-3	1-0	0-1	1-2	1-3	5-0	1-2	2-2	1-3	3-0	1-1		1-4	1-1
WEST HAM UTD	0-0	0-0	1-2	1-0	3-2	0-1	2-1	0-1	1-2	3-1	2-2	2-4	3-3	2-0	0-4	0-0	2-0	3-3	0-0	1-3		0-2
WIMBLEDON	0-3	2-2	4-1	1-1	1-2	1-1	0-2	1-0	1-1	1-0	1-0	4-2	3-1	3-0	1-1	2-0	2-1	1-0	3-0	2-1	1-2	

Manchester Utd.	42	27	11	4	80	38	92
Blackburn Rvrs.	42	25	9	8	63	36	84
Newcastle United	42	23	8	11	82	41	77
Arsenal	42	18	17	7	53	28	71
Leeds United	42	18	16	8	65	39	70
Wimbledon	42	18	11	13	56	53	65
Sheffield W'day	42	16	16	10	76	54	64
Liverpool	42	17	9	16	59	55	60
Q.P.R.	42	16	12	14	62	61	60
Aston Villa	42	15	12	15	46	50	57
Coventry City	42	14	14	14	43	45	56
Norwich City	42	12	17	13	65	61	53
West Ham United	42	13	13	16	47	58	52
Chelsea	42	13	12	17	49	53	51
Tott'ham Hotspur	42	11	12	19	54	59	45
Manchester City	42	9	18	15	38	49	45
Everton	42	12	8	22	42	63	44
Southampton	42	12	7	23	49	66	43
Ipswich Town	42	9	16	17	35	58	43
Sheffield United	42	8	18	16	42	60	42
Oldham Athletic	42	9	13	20	42	68	40
Swindon Town	42	5	15	22	47	100	30

Champions : - Manchester United

Relegated : - Sheffield United, Oldham Athletic and Swindon Town

1st Division — Season 1993/94

Results grid (home team in left column, away team across the top). Column codes: BAR = Barnsley, BIR = Birmingham C., BOL = Bolton W., BRI = Bristol C., CHA = Charlton A., CRY = Cry. Palace, DER = Derby Co., GRI = Grimsby T., LEI = Leicester, LUT = Luton Town, MID = Middlesbr., MIL = Millwall, NTF = Nottm. For., NTC = Notts Co., OXF = Oxford Utd, PET = Peterboro, POR = Portsmth, SOU = Southend, STO = Stoke City, SUN = Sund'land, TRA = Tranmere, WAT = Watford, WBA = West Brom., WOL = Wolves.

	BAR	BIR	BOL	BRI	CHA	CRY	DER	GRI	LEI	LUT	MID	MIL	NTF	NTC	OXF	PET	POR	SOU	STO	SUN	TRA	WAT	WBA	WOL
BARNSLEY	■	2-3	1-1	1-1	0-1	1-3	0-1	1-2	0-1	1-0	1-4	0-1	1-0	0-3	1-0	1-0	2-0	1-3	3-0	4-0	1-0	0-1	1-1	2-0
BIRMINGHAM C.	0-2	■	2-1	2-2	1-0	2-4	3-0	1-1	0-3	1-1	1-0	1-0	0-3	2-3	1-1	0-0	0-1	3-1	3-1	0-0	0-3	1-0	2-0	2-2
BOLTON WANDS.	2-3	1-1	■	2-2	3-2	1-0	0-2	1-1	1-2	2-1	4-1	4-3	4-2	1-0	1-1	1-1	0-2	1-1	0-0	2-1	3-1	1-1	1-3	
BRISTOL CITY	0-2	3-0	2-0	■	0-0	2-0	0-0	1-0	1-3	1-0	0-0	2-2	1-4	0-2	0-1	4-1	1-0	2-1	0-0	2-0	2-0	1-1	0-0	2-1
CHARLTON ATH.	2-1	1-0	3-0	3-1	■	0-0	1-2	0-1	2-1	1-0	2-5	0-0	0-1	5-1	1-0	5-1	0-0	4-3	2-0	0-0	3-1	2-1	2-1	0-1
CRYST. PALACE	1-0	2-1	1-1	4-1	2-0	■	1-1	1-0	2-1	3-2	0-1	1-0	2-0	1-2	2-1	3-2	5-1	1-0	4-1	1-0	0-2	1-0	1-1	
DERBY COUNTY	2-0	1-1	2-0	1-0	0-2	3-1	■	2-1	3-2	2-1	1-0	0-2	1-1	2-1	1-0	1-3	4-2	5-0	4-0	1-2	5-3	0-4		
GRIMSBY TOWN	2-2	1-0	0-0	1-0	0-1	1-1	1-1	■	0-0	2-0	1-1	0-0	0-0	2-2	1-0	3-1	1-1	4-0	0-0	0-1	0-0	2-2	2-2	2-0
LEICESTER CITY	0-1	1-1	1-1	3-0	2-1	1-1	3-3	1-1	■	2-1	4-0	1-0	3-2	2-3	2-1	0-3	3-0	1-1	2-1	1-1	4-4	4-2	2-2	
LUTON TOWN	5-0	1-1	0-2	0-2	1-0	0-1	2-1	2-1	0-2	■	1-1	1-1	1-2	1-0	3-0	2-0	4-1	1-1	6-2	1-1	1-1	3-2	1-0	
MIDDLESBRO'	5-0	2-2	0-1	0-1	1-0	2-3	3-0	1-0	2-0	0-0	■	4-2	2-2	3-0	2-1	1-0	0-2	1-0	2-1	4-1	0-0	1-1	3-0	1-0
MILLWALL	2-0	2-1	1-0	0-0	2-1	3-0	0-0	1-0	0-0	2-2	1-1	■	2-2	2-0	2-2	1-0	0-0	1-4	2-0	2-1	3-1	4-1	2-1	1-0
NOTT. FOREST	2-1	1-0	3-2	0-0	1-1	1-1	1-1	5-3	4-0	2-0	1-1	1-3	■	1-0	0-0	2-0	1-1	2-0	2-3	2-2	2-1	2-1	2-1	0-0
NOTTS COUNTY	3-1	2-1	2-1	2-0	3-3	3-2	4-1	2-1	4-1	1-2	2-3	1-3	2-1	■	2-1	1-2	1-0	2-1	2-0	1-0	0-0	1-0	1-0	0-2
OXFORD UTD.	1-1	2-0	0-2	4-2	0-4	1-3	2-0	2-2	2-2	0-1	1-1	0-2	1-0	2-1	■	1-2	3-2	2-1	1-0	0-3	1-0	2-3	1-1	4-0
PETERBORO' U.	4-1	1-0	2-3	0-2	0-1	1-1	2-2	1-2	1-1	0-0	0-0	2-3	1-1	3-1		■	2-2	3-1	1-1	1-3	0-0	3-4	2-0	0-1
PORTSMOUTH	2-1	0-2	0-0	0-0	1-2	0-1	3-2	3-1	0-1	1-0	2-0	2-2	2-1	0-0	1-1	0-2	■	2-1	3-3	0-1	2-0	2-0	0-1	3-0
SOUTHEND UTD.	0-3	3-1	0-2	0-1	4-2	1-2	4-3	1-2	0-1	1-1	1-1	1-1	1-0	6-1	3-0	2-1		■	0-0	0-1	1-2	2-0	0-3	1-1
STOKE CITY	5-4	2-1	2-0	3-0	1-0	0-2	2-1	1-0	2-2	3-1	2-4	3-1	1-1	2-0	0-1	2-0	1-0	1-2	■	2-0	1-1			
SUNDERLAND	1-0	1-0	2-0	0-0	4-0	1-0	1-0	2-2	2-3	2-0	2-1	2-2	1-2	2-3	2-0	2-0	1-2	0-2	0-1	■	3-2	2-0	1-0	0-2
TRANMERE R.	0-3	1-2	2-1	2-2	2-0	0-1	4-0	1-2	1-0	4-1	4-0	3-2	1-2	3-1	2-0	2-1	3-1	1-1	2-0	4-1	■	2-1	3-0	1-1
WATFORD	0-2	5-2	4-3	1-1	2-2	1-3	3-4	0-3	1-1	2-2	2-2	2-1	1-0	3-0	1-3	1-1	1-2					■	0-1	1-0
WEST BROM. A.	1-1	2-4	2-2	0-1	2-0	1-4	1-2	1-0	1-2	1-1	1-1	0-2	0-0	3-0	3-1	4-1	2-2	0-0	3-0	1-3	4-1		■	3-2
WOLVES	1-1	3-0	1-0	3-1	1-1	2-0	2-2	0-0	1-1	1-0	2-3	2-0	1-1	3-0	2-1	1-1	1-1	0-1	1-1	1-1	2-1	2-0	1-2	■

Final Table

Team	P	W	D	L	F	A	Pts
Crystal Palace	46	27	9	10	73	46	90
Nott'ham Forest	46	23	14	9	74	49	83
Millwall	46	19	17	10	58	49	74
Leicester City	46	19	16	11	72	59	73
Tranmere Rovers	46	21	9	16	69	53	72
Derby County	46	20	11	15	73	68	71
Notts County	46	20	7	9	65	69	68
Wolver'ton Wand.	46	17	17	12	60	47	68
Middlesbrough	46	18	13	15	66	54	67
Stoke City	46	18	13	15	57	59	67
Charlton Athletic	46	19	8	19	61	58	65
Sunderland	46	19	8	19	54	57	65
Bristol City	46	16	16	14	47	50	64
Bolton Wands.	46	15	14	17	63	64	59
Southend United	46	17	8	21	63	67	59
Grimsby Town	46	13	20	13	52	47	59
Portsmouth	46	15	13	18	52	58	58
Barnsley	46	16	7	23	55	67	55
Watford	46	15	9	22	66	80	54
Luton Town	46	14	11	21	56	60	53
West Brom. Alb.	46	13	12	21	60	69	51
Birmingham City	46	13	11	12	42	69	51
Oxford United	46	13	10	23	54	75	49
Peterboro' Utd.	46	8	13	25	48	76	37

PROMOTION PLAY-OFFS

Derby County 2	Millwall 0
Tranmere Rovers 0	Leicester City 0

Millwall... 1 — Derby County 3
Derby County win 5-1 on aggregate
Leicester City .... 2 — Tranmere Rovers 1
Leicester City win 2-1 on aggregate

Derby County .... 1 — Leicester City 2

Promoted : - Crystal Palace, Nottingham Forest & Leicester City

Relegated : - Birmingham City, Oxford United & Peterborough United

2nd Division Season 1993/94

	BARNET	BLACKPOOL	BOURNE TH.	BRADFORD	BRENTFORD	BRIGHTON	BRISTOL R.	BURNLEY	CAMBRIDGE	CARDIFF C.	EXETER CITY	FULHAM	HARTLEPOOL	HUDDFIELD	HULL CITY	LEYTON OR.	PLYMOUTH	PORT VALE	READING	ROTHERHAM	STOCKPORT	SWANSEA C.	WREXHAM	YORK CITY
BARNET	⬛	0-1	1-2	1-2	0-0	1-1	1-2	1-1	2-3	0-0	2-1	0-2	3-2	0-1	1-2	3-1	0-0	2-3	0-1	2-1	0-0	0-1	1-2	1-3
BLACKPOOL	3-1	⬛	2-1	1-3	1-1	2-0	0-1	1-2	2-3	1-0	1-0	2-3	2-1	2-1	6-2	4-1	2-1	1-3	0-4	1-2	2-0	1-1	4-1	0-5
BOURNEMOUTH	1-1	1-0	⬛	1-1	0-3	2-1	3-0	1-0	1-2	3-2	1-1	1-3	0-0	1-2	0-2	1-1	0-1	2-1	2-1	0-0	1-1	0-1	1-2	3-1
BRADFORD CITY	2-1	2-1	0-0	⬛	1-0	2-0	0-1	0-1	2-0	2-0	6-0	0-0	2-1	3-0	1-1	0-0	1-5	2-1	2-4	2-1	1-2	2-1	1-0	0-0
BRENTFORD	1-0	3-0	1-1	2-0	⬛	1-1	3-4	0-0	3-3	1-1	2-1	1-2	1-0	1-2	0-3	0-1	1-1	1-2	1-0	2-2	1-1	1-1	2-1	1-1
BRIGHTON & H.A.	1-0	3-2	3-3	0-1	2-1	⬛	0-2	1-1	4-1	3-5	0-0	2-0	1-1	2-2	3-0	2-0	1-3	0-1	0-2	1-1	4-1	1-1	2-0	
BRISTOL RVRS.	5-2	1-0	0-1	4-3	1-4	1-0	⬛	3-1	2-1	2-1	1-1	2-1	1-1	0-0	1-1	1-1	0-0	2-0	1-1	0-2	1-1	1-2	3-1	0-1
BURNLEY	5-0	3-1	4-0	0-1	4-1	3-0	3-1	⬛	3-0	2-0	3-2	3-1	2-0	1-1	3-1	4-1	4-2	2-1	0-1	0-0	1-1	1-1	2-1	2-1
CAMBRIDGE UTD	1-1	3-2	3-2	2-1	1-1	2-1	1-3	0-1	⬛	1-1	3-0	3-0	1-0	4-5	3-4	3-1	2-0	1-0	0-1	0-1	0-0	2-0	2-2	0-2
CARDIFF CITY	0-0	0-2	2-1	1-1	1-1	2-2	1-2	2-1	2-7	⬛	2-0	1-0	2-2	2-2	3-4	2-0	2-3	1-3	3-0	1-0	3-1	1-0	5-1	0-0
EXETER CITY	0-0	1-0	0-2	0-0	2-2	1-1	1-0	4-1	0-5	2-2	⬛	6-4	2-1	2-3	0-1	1-0	2-3	1-1	4-6	1-1	1-2	1-0	5-0	1-2
FULHAM	3-0	1-0	0-2	1-1	0-0	0-1	0-1	3-2	0-2	1-3	0-2	⬛	2-0	1-1	0-1	2-3	1-1	0-0	1-0	1-0	0-1	3-1	0-0	0-1
HARTLEPOOL	2-1	2-0	1-1	1-2	0-1	2-2	2-1	4-1	0-2	3-0	1-2	0-1	⬛	1-4	0-1	1-1	1-8	1-4	1-4	2-0	1-0	1-0	1-2	0-2
HUDDERSFIELD	1-2	2-1	1-1	1-1	1-3	1-3	1-0	1-1	1-1	2-0	0-1	1-0	1-1	⬛	0-2	1-0	1-0	1-1	0-3	2-1	1-1	1-1	3-0	3-2
HULL CITY	4-4	0-0	1-1	3-1	1-0	0-0	3-0	1-2	2-0	1-0	5-1	1-1	1-0	2-1	⬛	0-1	2-2	0-0	1-2	4-1	0-1	0-0	0-0	1-1
LEYTON ORIENT	4-2	2-0	0-0	2-1	1-1	1-3	1-0	3-1	2-1	2-2	1-1	2-2	1-2	1-0	3-1	⬛	2-1	2-3	1-1	1-1	0-0	2-1	2-2	2-0
PLYMOUTH ARG.	1-0	2-1	2-0	3-1	1-1	1-1	3-3	3-2	0-3	1-2	1-0	3-1	2-0	2-0	2-1	3-1	⬛	2-0	3-1	4-2	2-3	2-1	1-1	2-1
PORT VALE	6-0	2-0	2-1	0-0	1-0	4-0	2-0	1-1	2-2	2-2	3-0	2-2	1-0	1-0	2-1	2-1	2-1	⬛	0-4	2-1	1-1	3-0	3-0	2-1
READING	4-1	1-1	3-0	1-1	2-1	2-0	2-0	2-1	3-1	1-0	1-0	4-0	0-0	1-1	2-1	3-2	1-2		⬛	0-0	2-0	2-1	0-1	2-1
ROTHERHAM U.	1-1	0-2	1-2	2-1	2-0	0-1	1-1	3-2	3-0	5-2	3-0	1-2	7-0	1-0	2-1	0-3	0-2	2-2		⬛	1-2	1-1	2-1	2-1
STOCKPORT CO.	2-1	1-0	0-2	4-1	3-1	3-0	0-2	2-1	3-1	2-2	4-0	2-4	5-0	3-0	0-0	3-0	2-3	2-1	1-1	2-0	⬛	4-0	1-0	1-3
SWANSEA CITY	2-0	4-4	1-1	2-0	1-1	3-0	2-0	3-1	4-2	1-0	2-0	1-1	1-0	1-1	0-1	0-1	1-1	0-0	1-2			⬛	3-1	1-2
WREXHAM	4-0	2-3	2-1	0-3	1-2	1-3	3-2	1-0	1-1	3-1	1-1	2-0	2-0	3-1	3-0	4-2	0-3	2-1	3-2	3-3	0-1	3-2	⬛	1-1
YORK CITY	1-1	2-1	2-0	1-1	0-2	3-1	0-1	0-0	2-0	5-0	3-0	2-0	3-0	0-2	0-0	3-0	0-0	1-0	1-0	0-0	1-2	2-1	1-1	⬛

	P	W	D	L	F	A	Pts
Reading	46	26	11	9	81	44	89
Port Vale	46	26	10	10	79	46	88
Plymouth Argyle	46	25	10	11	88	56	85
Stockport Co.	46	24	13	9	74	44	85
York City	46	21	12	13	64	40	75
Burnley	46	21	10	15	79	58	73
Bradford City	46	19	13	14	61	53	70
Bristol Rovers	46	20	10	16	60	59	70
Hull City	46	18	14	14	62	54	68
Cambridge Utd.	46	19	9	18	79	73	66
Huddersfield Tn.	46	17	14	15	58	61	65
Wrexham	46	17	11	18	66	77	62
Swansea City	46	16	12	18	56	58	60
Brighton & H.A.	46	15	14	17	60	67	59
Rotherham Utd.	46	15	13	18	63	60	58
Brentford	46	13	19	14	57	55	58
Bournemouth	46	14	15	17	51	59	57
Leyton Orient	46	14	14	18	57	71	56
Cardiff City	46	13	15	18	66	79	54
Blackpool	46	16	5	25	63	75	53
Fulham	46	14	10	22	50	63	52
Exeter City	46	11	12	23	52	83	45
Harltepool Utd.	46	9	9	28	41	87	36
Barnet	46	5	13	28	41	86	28

PROMOTION PLAY-OFFS

Burnley 0	Plymouth Argyle 0
York City 0	Stockport County 0

Plymouth Argyle 1	Burnley 3

Burnley win 3-1 on aggregate

Stockport County 1	York City 0

West Bromwich Albion win 1-0 on aggregate

Burnley 2	Stockport County 1

Promoted : - Reading, Port Vale & Burnley

Relegated : - Fulham, Exeter City, Hartlepool United & Barnet

3rd Division — Season 1993/94

	BURY	CARLISLE UTD.	CHESTER CITY	CHESTERFIELD	COLCHESTER U.	CREWE ALEX.	DARLINGTON	DONCASTER R.	GILLINGHAM	HEREFORD UTD.	LINCOLN CITY	MANSFIELD T.	NORTHAMPTON	PRESTON N.E.	ROCHDALE	SCARBOROUGH	SCUNTHORPE U.	SHREWSBURY T.	TORQUAY UTD.	WALSALL	WIGAN ATHLETIC	WYCOMBE W.
BURY		2-1	1-1	2-1	0-1	1-0	5-1	4-0	0-0	5-3	1-0	2-2	0-0	1-1	0-1	0-2	1-0	2-3	1-1	1-2	3-0	1-2
CARLISLE UTD.	1-2		1-0	3-0	2-0	1-2	2-0	4-2	1-2	1-2	3-3	1-1	0-1	0-1	0-1	2-0	3-1	2-1	1-1	2-1	3-0	2-2
CHESTER CITY	3-0	0-0		3-1	2-1	1-2	0-0	0-1	1-0	3-1	1-1	1-1	1-0	3-2	3-1	4-1	0-2	1-0	1-1	2-1	2-1	3-1
CHESTERFIELD	1-1	3-0	1-2		0-0	2-0	1-1	1-1	3-2	3-1	2-2	0-2	4-0	1-1	1-1	1-0	1-1	1-2	3-1	0-1	1-0	2-3
COLCHESTER U.	4-1	2-1	0-0	0-2		2-4	1-2	3-1	1-2	1-0	1-0	0-0	3-2	1-1	2-5	1-2	2-1	3-3	1-2	0-1	3-1	0-2
CREWE ALEX.	2-4	2-3	2-1	0-1	2-1		2-1	2-0	1-0	6-0	2-2	2-1	3-1	4-3	2-1	1-1	3-3	0-3	0-2	1-2	4-1	2-1
DARLINGTON	1-0	1-3	1-2	0-0	7-3	1-0		1-3	2-1	1-3	3-2	2-0	0-1	0-2	1-1	0-2	2-1	0-2	1-2	0-0	0-0	0-0
DONCASTER R.	1-3	0-0	3-4	0-0	2-1	0-0	1-3		0-0	1-0	1-0	0-1	2-1	1-1	2-1	0-4	3-1	0-0	0-2	4-0	3-1	0-3
GILLINGHAM	1-0	2-0	2-2	0-2	3-0	1-3	2-1	0-0		2-0	1-1	1-0	1-0	2-2	1-2	2-2	1-0	0-2	2-2	1-1	2-2	0-1
HEREFORD UTD.	3-0	1-1	0-5	0-3	5-0	1-2	1-1	2-1	2-0		1-2	2-3	1-1	2-3	5-1	1-1	1-2	0-1	2-0	1-1	3-0	3-4
LINCOLN CITY	2-2	0-0	0-3	1-2	2-0	1-2	1-1	2-1	3-1	3-1		1-2	4-3	0-2	1-1	0-1	2-0	1-1	1-0	1-2	0-1	1-3
MANSFIELD T.	2-2	0-1	0-4	1-2	1-1	1-2	0-3	2-1	2-1	2-1	1-0		1-0	2-2	0-1	4-2	0-1	1-0	2-1	1-2	2-3	3-0
NORTHAMPTON	0-1	1-1	1-0	2-2	1-1	2-2	1-0	0-0	1-2	0-1	0-0	5-1		2-0	1-2	3-2	4-0	0-3	0-1	0-1	0-2	1-1
PRESTON N.E.	3-1	0-3	1-1	4-1	1-0	0-2	3-2	3-1	0-0	3-0	2-0	3-1	1-1		2-1	2-2	2-2	6-1	3-1	2-0	3-0	2-3
ROCHDALE	2-1	0-1	2-0	5-1	1-1	2-1	0-0	1-1	3-0	2-0	0-1	1-1	6-2	2-1		2-1	2-3	1-2	4-1	0-0	1-2	2-2
SCARBOROUGH	1-0	0-3	0-1	1-1	0-2	1-2	3-0	2-0	1-1	0-1	2-2	1-1	2-1	3-4	2-1		0-1	1-3	1-2	1-0	4-1	3-1
SCUNTHORPE U.	1-1	2-1	1-1	2-2	1-1	2-1	3-0	1-3	1-1	1-2	2-0	2-3	7-0	3-1	2-1	1-1		1-4	1-3	5-0	1-0	0-0
SHREWSBURY T.	1-0	1-0	3-0	0-0	2-1	2-2	1-1	0-1	2-2	2-0	2-2	2-2	2-1	1-0	1-1	2-0	0-0		3-2	1-2	0-0	1-1
TORQUAY UTD.	0-0	1-1	1-3	1-0	3-3	3-3	2-1	2-1	0-1	1-1	3-2	1-0	2-0	4-3	1-1	2-0	1-1	0-0		0-1	1-1	1-1
WALSALL	0-1	0-1	1-1	0-1	1-2	2-2	3-0	1-2	1-0	3-3	5-2	0-2	1-3	2-0	1-0	1-0	0-0	0-1	1-2		1-1	4-2
WIGAN ATH.	3-1	0-2	6-3	1-0	0-1	2-2	2-0	0-0	2-0	3-4	0-1	4-1	1-1	2-2	0-0	1-2	0-2	2-5	1-3	2-2		1-1
WYCOMBE W.	2-1	2-0	1-0	0-1	2-5	3-1	2-0	1-0	3-2	2-3	1-0	1-0	1-1	1-1	4-0	2-2	1-1	1-1	3-0	0-1		

	P	W	D	L	F	A	Pts
Shrewsbury Tn.	42	22	13	7	63	39	79
Chester City	42	21	11	10	69	46	74
Crewe Alex.	42	21	10	11	80	61	73
Wycombe Wands.	42	19	13	10	67	53	70
Preston N. E.	42	18	13	11	79	60	67
Torquay United	42	17	16	9	64	56	67
Carlisle United	42	18	10	14	57	42	64
Chesterfield	42	16	14	12	55	48	62
Rochdale	42	16	12	14	63	51	60
Walsall	42	17	9	16	48	53	60
Scunthorpe Utd.	42	15	14	13	64	56	59
Mansfield Town	42	15	10	17	53	62	55
Bury	42	14	11	17	55	56	53
Scarborough	42	15	8	19	55	61	53
Doncaster Rvrs.	42	14	10	18	44	57	52
Gillingham	42	12	15	14	44	51	51
Colchester Utd.	42	13	10	19	56	71	49
Lincoln City	42	12	11	19	52	63	47
Wigan Athletic	42	11	12	19	51	70	45
Hereford United	42	12	6	24	60	79	42
Darlington	42	10	11	21	42	64	41
Northampton Tn.	42	9	11	22	44	66	38

PROMOTION PLAY-OFFS

Carlisle United 0   Wycombe Wanderers............2
Torquay United........................2   Preston North End 0

Wycombe Wanderers 2   Carlisle United......................1
Wycombe Wanderers win 4-1 on aggregate
Preston North End 4   Torquay United 1
Preston North End win 4-3 on aggregate

Wycombe Wanderers 4   Preston North End 2

Promoted : - Shrewsbury Town, Chester City, Crewe Alexandra & Wycombe Wanderers

Relegated : - No relegation

The 92 Club

The 92 Club was founded in June 1978 with an initial membership of 39. Its purpose was to bring together football followers who have watched matches at all the 92 league grounds. The number of fans who have achieved this goal has steadily increased over the years and we now boast a membership approaching 900. However, with a number of new stadiums having been built in recent years, and a few more possibly in the pipeline, coupled with the automatic promotion from the GM Vauxhall Conference league of one club each season, it is likely one would have visited up to 100 stadia or more to complete the '92'.

The club is a non-profit making organisation and any qualifiers wishing to join the club would pay a small joining fee which will include a certificate as confirmation of completion together with an exclusive 92 Club metal badge and current newsletter. The club also stocks a range of souvenirs such as scarfs, ties, mugs, pencils and a rather neat personalised trophy. The club also produces a "Complete Statistical Record Book" at £2.00 including P&P to help the dedicated fan keep a record of games attended and includes space for line-ups, substitutions, scorers, bookings, officials, attendance and even the weather!

To help bring together fans across the country the club meet on a number of occasions throughout the season at selected matches, and games that prove to be particularly attractive are first/last game for a club at its stadium or indeed in the league. These meetings usually prove popular and are a good way to make friends and exchange stories with fellow fans. The club also arrange matchball sponsorship from time to time and stadium tours etc. which prove enjoyable.

The majority of fans follow a particular club and all clubs in the Premiership and Football League have members of the 92 Club except one, that being Crewe Alexandra, so if there are any Crewe fans who've done them all why not join this exclusive band of supporters? At the other end of the scale, Oxford United have most fans in our club with 20 members but others such as Tottenham, Aston Villa and Brighton are hot on their tails. Torquay United's Plainmoor ground appears to be the most popular to finish at - a nice sunny end of season game at the seaside perhaps!!

The club has also attracted quite a lot of attention in recent years and has appeared on national television on a number of occasions, but perhaps the highlight was being contacted by the BBC to appear on the Noel Edmonds series "Noel's Addicts" in 1992.

If any readers have completed the current 92 Premier and Football League grounds and have not yet joined the club, why not send a s.a.e. to the address below for joining details. If any of the above has whetted the appetite of fans who wish to complete the lot at some stage in the future and you want more information, again, please write and we'll be happy to provide information for you. The address is: The 92 Club, 104 Gilda Crescent, Whitchurch, Bristol, BS14 9LD.

THE SHOOT!
DISABLED SUPPORTERS'
GUIDE TO
BRITISH FOOTBALL
1995

Previous editions of our Supporters' Guides have contained limited information for disabled fans - limited because of space restrictions. In conjunction with Shoot! magazine, we are, therefore, publishing an entirely separate guide for disabled fans which provides extended information for the top League and Non-League clubs in the country (not just the 92 'English' clubs).

Sample entries are shown below: -

ASTON VILLA FC

WHEELCHAIRS :	**Location of Accommodation**: Special Section - Trinity Road Stand
	N° Spaces for Home Fans; **N° Spaces for Away Fans**: 40 Spaces in total
	Are Helpers Admitted; **N° Admitted**: By letter of request of disabled - one per disabled fan.
PRICES :	**Prices for Disabled**; **Prices for Helpers**: At Club's discretion for disabled. Helpers full price.
TOILETS :	**Location of Disabled Toilets (+ Number)**: One in Trinity Road Stand
BLIND :	**Facilities Available**: Commentaries by Arrangement
BOOKINGS :	**Are Bookings Necessary**: Yes **CONTACT NUMBER**: (021) 327-2299

YORK CITY FC

WHEELCHAIRS :	**Location of Accommodation**: Accommodated in Disabled Section - In front of Family Stand
	N° Spaces for Home Fans; **N° Spaces for Away Fans**: 18 spaces available in total
	Are Helpers Admitted; **N° Admitted**: One helper admitted per disabled person
PRICES :	**Prices for Disabled**; **Prices for Helpers**: Free of charge for the disabled. Helpers £6.50
TOILETS :	**Location of Disabled Toilets (+ Number)**: Available at entrance to Disabled Area
BLIND :	**Facilities Available**: Commentaries Available
BOOKINGS :	**Are Bookings Necessary**: No **CONTACT NUMBER**: (0904) 624447

The guide can be obtained from all good bookshops or directly from Soccer Book Publishing priced 99p per copy + 30p postage.

Other Supporters' Guides : -

THE SUPPORTERS' GUIDE TO NON-LEAGUE FOOTBALL 1995

Featuring :
- all GM/Vauxhall Conference clubs
- all Northern Premier clubs
- all Beazer Homes - Premier clubs
- all Diadora Premier clubs
+ 180 other major Non-League clubs
112 pages - price £4.99 - post free

THE SUPPORTERS' GUIDE TO SCOTTISH FOOTBALL 1995

Featuring :
- all Scottish League clubs
- all Highland League clubs
- all East & South of Scotland League clubs
+ Results, tables
96 pages - price £4.99 - post free

THE SUPPORTERS' GUIDE TO WELSH FOOTBALL 1995

Featuring :
- all Konica League of Wales clubs
- all Cymru Alliance clubs
- all Welsh Football League clubs
+ 'The Exiles', Minor League clubs & 1993/94 season's results and tables
96 pages - price £4.99 - post free

order from : -

**SOCCER BOOK PUBLISHING LTD.
DEPT. SBP
72 ST. PETERS AVENUE
CLEETHORPES
DN35 8HU
ENGLAND**

72 St. Peters Avenue, Cleethorpes, DN35 8HU, England
24hr orderline (0472) 696226
Faxline (0472) 698546

VHS only

ALL PRICES INCLUDE POSTAGE

UK : **1st Class Letter Post**

Overseas : **Airmail Post**

10% DISCOUNT
ON ALL ORDERS
IN EXCESS OF £60.00

UK - FORMAT VIDEOS (Suitable for UK, Europe & Australasia)

OFFICIAL HIGHLIGHTS OF THE SEASON

All priced :   £13.99 UK ;   £17.99 Overseas *(including postage)*

1993/94

Arsenal	Aston Villa	Chelsea
Everton	Leeds United	Liverpool
Manchester City	Manchester United	Sheff. Wednesday
Ipswich Town	Newcastle United	Blackburn Rovers
Nottingham Forest	West Ham United	Leicester City

THE GOLDEN GOALS COLLECTION

All priced :   £11.99 UK ;   £15.99 Overseas *(including postage)*

Arsenal	Aston Villa	Blackburn
Chelsea	Coventry City	Everton
Ipswich Town	Leeds United	Liverpool
Manchester City	Manchester United	Newcastle United
Norwich City	Queen's Park Rangers	Oldham Athletic
Rangers (Glasgow)	Sheffield Wednesday	Sheffield United
Southampton	Swindon Town	Tottenham Hotspur
West Ham United	Wimbledon	

Order From : **The Soccer Bookshelf (Dept SBP)**
72 St. Peters Avenue, Cleethorpes, DN35 8HU, England
Pay By : **Cash/Cheque/Postal Order or**
Credit Card : Access/Mastercard/Barclaycard/Visa/Amex

THE COMPLETE RECORD SERIES

This highly-acclaimed series of Hardback Club histories contains a full record of
results, line-ups, attendances, scorers, managers and players' profiles.
Each priced £16.95 unless otherwise shown. Postage UK +£3.50; Overseas +£5.50; Air +£10.50

Accrington Stanley 1894-1962; Blackpool 1887-1992; Coventry 1883-1991; Derby County 1884-1988 (£14.95); Everton 1878-1993; Exeter City 1904-1990 (£14,95); Hull City 1904-1989 (£14,95); Manchester City 1887-1993; Middlesbrough 1876-1993; Millwall 1885-1991; New Brighton (£12.95); Nottingham Forest 1865-1991; Oldham Athletic 1907-1988 (£14.95); Oxford United 1893-1989 (£14.95); Q.P.R. 1882-1993; Saints (Southampton) 1885-1987 (£15.95); Spurs 1882-1993; West Bromwich Albion 1879-1993; West Ham United 1895-1993; Wrexham 1873-1992; York City 1922-1990.

OTHER TITLES

THE AEROFILMS GUIDE TO FOOTBALL LEAGUE GROUNDS 2nd EDITION
Featuring full-colour aerial photos of every F.A. Premier and Football League Ground.
Softback Price £10.99   Postage :   UK + £1.50 ;   Overseas + £2.50 ;   Airmail + £4.50

BRITISH FOOTBALL GROUNDS THEN AND NOW
Featuring old black and white aerial photos alongside current shots.
Hardback Price £14.99   Postage :   UK + £3.50 ;   Overseas + £5.50 ;   Airmail + £8.00

THE BREEDON BOOK OF FOOTBALL LEAGUE RECORDS
An excellent book containing every result and league table.
Hardback Price £16.95   Postage :   UK + £3.50 ;   Overseas + £5.50 ;   Airmail + £10.50

Order From : **The Soccer Bookshelf (Dept SBP)**
72 St. Peters Avenue, Cleethorpes, DN35 8HU, England
Pay By : **Cash/Cheque/Postal Order or**
Credit Card : Access/Mastercard/Barclaycard/Visa/Amex

New titles available in
The 10 Seasons Series: -

MANCHESTER UNITED -
10 SEASONS AT OLD TRAFFORD
1984-85 to 1993-94

LIVERPOOL -
10 SEASONS AT ANFIELD
1984-85 to 1993-94

Complete Statistical Histories with: -
- Line-ups
- Scores
- Scorers
- Attendances
- Season-by-season write-ups
- Full players' directory

Each priced £4.99 - post free

Last season's titles available at HALF-PRICE: -

Barnsley .... *Seasons 1983-84 to 1992-93*
Grimsby Town .... *Seasons 1983-84 to 1992-93*
Leeds United .... *Seasons 1983-84 to 1992-93*
Newcastle United ...... *Seasons 1983-84 to 1992-93*
Scunthorpe United ... *Seasons 1983-84 to 1992-93*
Sunderland .... *Seasons 1983-84 to 1992-93*

Each priced £2.49 - post free

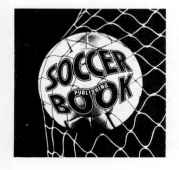

STOP MESSING ABOUT

BUY

ISBN 0-947808-36-

90minutes

THE FOOTBALL WEEKLY THAT CLEANS UP!

EVERY TUESDAY

ACCEPT NO SUBSTIT

90minutes

BEYOND THE
PLAY-OFFS

World Cup USA94
TEAM PROFILES

CHAMPIONS?

TWO UNLIMITED

PLUS

YOUNG,
GIFTED
& GREEN
IRELAND'S NEW
GENERATION